SIDE *by* SIDE

SIDE *by* SIDE

Women *and* Men
Leading Together *in the* Church

DAVE HESS

© Copyright 2020 – Dave Hess

All rights reserved. This book is protected by the copyright laws of the United States of America. This book may not be copied or reprinted for commercial gain or profit. The use of short quotations or occasional page copying for personal or group study is permitted and encouraged. Permission will be granted upon request. Scripture quotations are from the following versions of the Bible: New Revised Standard Version Bible, copyright © 1989 National Council of the Churches of Christ in the United States of America. Used by permission. All rights reserved worldwide. **THE HOLY BIBLE, NEW INTERNATIONAL VERSION®, NIV® Copyright © 1973, 1978, 1984, 2011 by Biblica, Inc.® Used by permission. All rights reserved worldwide.** Scripture quotations marked TPT are from The Passion Translation®. Copyright © 2017, 2018 by Passion & Fire Ministries, Inc. Used by permission. All rights reserved. ThePassionTranslation.com. Scripture taken from the NEW AMERICAN STANDARD BIBLE®, Copyright © 1960,1962,1963,1968,1971,1972,1973,1975,1977,1995 by The Lockman Foundation. Used by permission. Scripture quotations marked (ESV) are from The ESV® Bible (The Holy Bible, English Standard Version®), copyright © 2001 by Crossway, a publishing ministry of Good News Publishers. Used by permission. All rights reserved. Scripture quotations marked (KJV) are from The King James Version Bible. Scripture taken from the Holy Bible, NEW INTERNATIONAL READER'S VERSION®.Copyright © 1996, 1998 Biblica. All rights reserved throughout the world. Used by permission of Biblica.

Pagination and cover design by: Karen Webb

ISBN: 979-8-669190-96-5

For Worldwide Distribution, Printed in the U.S.A.

*To the sons and daughters:
May you freely be—all you were created to be.
May you fully do—all you were called to do.
And may you boldly go there—together.*

ACKNOWLEDGEMENTS

I'd like to thank those whose investment of time, energy, and encouragement made the completion of this book possible!

To Cindy Jacobs: You saw the stirring of God in my heart and called it forth. Huge thanks to you and Mike for pioneering and modeling what an honoring partnership looks like!

To Karen Webb: What a joy to work with you once again. Your creative skills have brought another dream into reality!

To Elise Jackson: You are a highly-gifted word artist. Your contribution to the continuity and accessibility of this text is unmistakable. Thank you for pouring your heart into this project!

To Monelle Baynard: Your gracious capacity for compassionate awareness and administrative resourcefulness is a joy to all who know you. Sheri and I are delighted to have you in our lives!

To Randy Clark and Tom Jones: Thank you for nudging me to return to school. Your hungry hearts continually stir me to pursue "the more!" I'm so grateful for all of your support, encouragement, and profound insights. You are a huge blessing to my life and to the body of Christ!

To my "Randy Clark's Scholars" cohorts—Ian Dunn, Marion Hayes, Barry Wissler, and Peter Young: I cherish our times of inspiring dialogue and challenging processing. Thank you for bringing fresh winds into my sails!

To our Christ Community family and our team of elders: I deeply appreciate your teachability, your flexibility, and your eagerness to embrace fresh understanding. You are forging a redemptive trail and preparing a life-giving legacy!

To my Sheri: Partnering with you is the greatest joy in my life. Your honesty, enthusiasm, courage, and compassion ceaselessly provoke me to aim higher! I love you more than words can express!

ENDORSEMENTS

I believe both sides of the issue concerning women in leadership in the church truly want to honor the Lord and follow His Word. Yet, so many are unwilling to have a meaningful dialogue about it. Looking only skin deep into the English language translations, it seems to say that women should not be leaders in the church. I am so grateful that there are male leaders in the body of Christ who have looked closely at the entirety of scripture in the original languages and are willing to address this controversy for all of us. Pastor Dave Hess is one of those men who is championing this issue with his preaching and the writing of his book, *Side by Side*. If you care about this topic at all and how it affects the body of Christ, this book is a must-read!

Anna Marie Dandy
Teacher, Leader, Elder
Christ Community Church
Camp Hill, PA

Dr. Hess' *Side by Side* will make a great impact on the church. It will set free numerous evangelicals and conservatives from the bondage of misconstrued biblical interpretations on women's leadership in the church. Jesus Christ came to restore the true image of God in both men and women. Jesus is the first Jewish Rabbi who made a woman his disciple by allowing Mary to sit at His feet for His teaching. Dr. Hess' work holds up men and women to build God's Kingdom together according to the image of God sealed in them. I wholeheartedly recommend Dr. Hess' book to all Christian leaders.

Dr. Andrew Park
Professor of Theology and Ethics
United Theological Seminary
Dayton, OH

Having grown up as a woman struggling to embrace my calling as a minister in churches that did not allow women to be in leadership, I wish I could have read this book many years ago. What I appreciate most is that Dr. Dave Hess thoroughly exegetes each of the scripture passages that are frequently quoted to keep women from taking leadership positions. This book reveals the heart of a pastor whose goal is not to start a debate, but who has a father's desire to empower women and men to come into their full calling. It is a precious gift to the

Church that will allow many women to freely step into all God created them to be.

Dr. Marion Hayes
Teacher, Leader
New York, NY

Side by Side is a piece of life offered as encouragement and thoughtful consideration. The topic isn't new and neither is the struggle. Finding a complementary process for men and women to minister together seems to elude church leaders. While we agree that men and women are equally valuable in the sight of the Lord, we wrestle with creating a "men's club" in church leadership again and again. Just as we would resist a single parent design for a family, we must also reject the idea that we can suitably respond to a congregation with a primarily male dominated leadership model. Dave and Sheri have worked for decades to find this rhythm. I am happy to recommend *Side by Side* as another room in the house God is building to change the way we lead in the Body of Christ.

Danny Silk
President of Loving on Purpose
Author of *Powerful & Free, Keep Your Love On, Unpunishable, Culture of Honor, Loving Our Kids on Purpose*
Sacramento, CA

Dr. Hess has done an outstanding job examining this subject with sound biblical scholarship. I am encouraging everyone to read *Side by Side,* especially leaders. We are living in the time when God said He would pour out His Spirit on all flesh and that sons and daughters will all speak for God, with no exclusions. The times we live in, and the waiting harvest, demand that men and women learn to lead together. You will enjoy and learn from this read. I know I did.

Dr. Barry Wissler
President, HarvestNet International
Ephrata, PA

Side by Side provides a bird's-eye view of an issue that has long been neglected—that of men and women in ministry together. In scripture, Jesus confronts the Pharisees time and again about their habit of nullifying scripture for the sake of tradition. Why? Because they refused to question their tradition. Paul, the Pharisee of Pharisees, one for whom tradition was everything, spent his entire ministry teaching, working with, and honoring women. Shouldn't such overwhelming evidence of a break with his tradition force us to re-examine how two scriptures are interpreted? It has been easier for us to simply ignore the issue and rest in our presuppositions than to challenge widely accepted tradition. Thank you, Pastor Dave, for taking us along with you on this challenging and profound journey toward the heart of the Father.

Therese Nehrt
Pastor, Teacher, Elder
Christ Community Church
Camp Hill, PA

Over the fifteen years that I've known David Hess, he has proven to be an incredible custodian of the call that God has placed on his life. He is a man of great integrity and compassion who leads with supernatural wisdom, sincere authenticity, and steadfast character.

In his new book, *Side-by-Side: Women and Men Leading Together in the Local Church,* Dave biblically confronts the lie of female inferiority—an issue the Body of Christ is called to address. With wisdom, Dave lends his voice to the complex conversation discussed within the Church about gender-exclusive roles and co-leading relationships between men and women. This book is an essential read for all leaders within the local church and any who are considering stepping into leadership roles.

Rightly proclaiming that God is "restoring everything we lost in Adam and Eve's revolt," Dave has woven God's heart for reconciliation throughout the pages of this valuable book. And he challenges you, the reader, to rise up and respond, bringing revival to callings gone dormant, and restoring authority that has been stolen from those God has called you to co-labor with! I highly recommend this book!

Kris Vallotton
Senior Leader, Bethel Church,
Redding, CA
Co-Founder of Bethel School of
Supernatural Ministry
Author of thirteen books, including
*The Supernatural Ways of Royalty,
Heavy Rain* and *Poverty, Riches and Wealth*

TABLE OF CONTENTS

FOREWORD. 17

PREFACE. 21

INTRODUCTION. 29

CHAPTER 1:
IN THE BEGINNING 31

CHAPTER 2:
**DISHARMONY, DISUNITY,
AND THE FALL OF HUMANITY** 47

CHAPTER 3:
**OLD TESTAMENT GLIMPSES OF THE
RESTORATION OF GOD'S ORIGINAL INTENT** 57

CHAPTER 4:
THE HIGH COST OF COMPROMISE 65

CHAPTER 5:
JESUS THE REVOLUTIONARY RESTORER 69

CHAPTER 6:
PIONEERING PARTNERSHIPS 75

CHAPTER 7:
DECLARATION OF INTERDEPENDENCE 85

CHAPTER 8:
1 TIMOTHY 2:11-15 IN CONTEXT 97

CHAPTER 9:
WHAT ABOUT THOSE OTHER VERSES? 113

CHAPTER 10:
A TALE OF TWO WOMEN 125

CHAPTER 11:
THEIR STORIES. 143

CHAPTER 12:
OUR STORY. 185

CHAPTER 13:
YOUR STORY 205

CHAPTER 14:
FINAL WORDS 215

ENDNOTES 219

FOREWORD

This is an extraordinary book! It's doubtless that the subject of men and women standing side by side in life and as ministers is going to be at the forefront in this new season for the church.

As I read these pages, I often thought, "I wish this book had been written thirty—almost forty—years ago, when I was grappling with this subject. It would have helped me so much!" You see, I have lived this story. When I first started preaching, I didn't know another woman in ministry.

Both Mike and I grew up with a church background that was loving toward women, but upheld a firm line saying that while women could teach Sunday School, they weren't supposed to teach men.

Oddly, when God thrust me out to preach at thirty years old, my husband had no theological problem with me following the call of God. We just had to work out who would keep up with the washing!

I, on the other hand, had issues. Lots of issues! This led me on a biblical search that culminated in the writing of my book *Women Rise Up* (originally, *Women of Destiny*). *Side by Side* goes further than what I wrote, because it includes how Dave Hess grappled with the issues he's faced as a man and a local pastor.

Women reading this book will feel supported. Those who've felt the sting of marginalization and pain from the rejection of their God-given gifts, will be comforted in knowing that one, brave man was willing to search for the truth of the scripture. A man truly needs to have courage to speak out on this subject, as many platforms remain closed to the female voice.

While reading this book, I thought back to when my husband and I lived in Colorado, and he received an invitation to a ministers' retreat which stated at the bottom: "Men Only." I also recalled the time a man stood up while I was preaching and shouted that my speaking as a woman was heretical. Then he dragged his wife out of the meeting. You might think, "Oh, that must have been years ago." Sadly, it wasn't.

This is the way of a pioneer. Someone once prayed for me that I would have the hide of a rhinoceros and the heart of a dove. I will say that, as a woman (at least at this time), one still needs to have pretty thick skin and a strong EQ.

I love the way that Dave honors his wife, and my friend, Sheri. She is exactly as he describes her: funny, loving, smart, and courageous. They have been forerunners in ministry for years. The generations that follow them will be rich because of their example of standing together, side by side.

It's my belief that many in the church are willing to grapple with the issue of men and women working together as partners. Maybe you're a leader and have found yourself praying into this subject. Dave has done excellent, honest research for you. He's vulnerable in his sharing with the reader, and doesn't gloss over the struggles that arose as he led his church in releasing women into leadership.

The Bible is clear that "in the beginning," a man and a woman were to be partners. With the introduction of the curse, a cycle of judgment began. But the good news is that the curse has been broken! We are the generation that's called to walk in freedom. The harvest is ripe! And we need all the laborers working side by side to bring it in.

Thank you, Dave, for writing this well-documented, insightful book. It will bring freedom to many!

Dr. Cindy Jacobs
Generals International
Dallas, Texas

PREFACE

As a man, I've lived in a partial cloud of denial, generally oblivious to the experiences of many women in my church culture. Marrying my wife and connecting with her world introduced me to a new paradigm. Sheri and I have been together for over 40 years. She's the extrovert of our team—a fully invested, life-of-the-party, never-met-a-stranger, organized and spontaneous trailblazer. She's a gifted teacher, encourager, and influencer. A few weeks into our marriage, Sheri was interviewed by the board of a parachurch ministry and was unanimously hired to serve as the administrator—a role she was well suited for. With youthful zeal we set up her office the next day, excited to see her utilize her gift-mix to serve others. However, our enthusiasm was short-lived. A pastor whose church gave significant financial support to the organization threatened to withdraw all funding if my wife continued as administrator. The solitary reason: Sheri is a woman. We chose to accept the decision of the board to terminate her on her first day of employment. Walking through that experience triggered suppressed memories, and I began to recall incidents of gender exclusion from my childhood and adolescent years in church-life.

In writing this book, I hope to contribute to the church's ongoing dialogue concerning the roles of men and women in leadership. What follows is an exploration of the scripture and invitation to discover God's original intent for His daughters and sons. Have men and women been designed to co-labor in every facet of authority? Or, has God assigned gender-exclusive roles and responsibilities, establishing strict boundaries without exception? Does the Bible clearly indicate that women and men can lead together? Or, do the scriptures forbid women from even considering such positions?

My personal journey regarding this subject continues to this day. Over my lifetime, I've evaluated my convictions, allowing them to be checked and challenged by the fresh perspectives of those I know, as well as by the many texts I've read. I invite you to ponder some of my discoveries and come to your own conclusions.

As a full-time pastor, much of my adult life has involved grappling with doctrinal matters. On this topic—the roles of women and men in church leadership over recent years—I've engaged in focused study. By the grace of God, the encouragement of my wife, and the prayerful support of close friends, I enrolled in the doctor of ministry studies at United Theological Seminary in Dayton, Ohio. My doctoral project was entitled *A Gender-Inclusive Leadership Environment in the Local Church*. It took me on a wonderful intensive journey of interaction with pastoral peers, interviews with men and women in church leadership, blind surveys of a wide array of local church members, and hours of research in studies by classic to contemporary Bible scholars. The opinions were varied, and some of the discussions were intense. Raw emotions mixing with resolute judgments can create passionate clashes! Conversations were at times tearful, and in other moments, joyful. In the end, all of my interactions brought clear confirmation: this is an issue that requires attention.

Currently, a number of books are being published to encourage prayerful consideration of this important subject. I write with similar objectives. Though I've come to some deeply settled personal convictions, my desire is to fairly present what my research uncovered. I encourage you to grapple with the issues. Face your fears. (I had plenty!) Examine your traditions. (I was steeped in mine!) Be willing to consider new views of familiar scriptures. And at all times, trust the Holy Spirit to faithfully lead us into more truth.

My early years were steeped in a Bible-believing, theologically conservative "church-family-of-origin," which provided me with good foundations and warm memories. But in the midst of many fond recollections, I recall one puzzling practice: some of the older men sat on the right-hand side of our sanctuary, while their wives sat on the other. In my early adolescence, I learned that this practice was reminiscent of days when the entire congregation observed this gender separation. An older gentleman (who continued to sit apart from his wife) explained that the Apostle Paul clearly commanded it: Women were to be seated separately from their husbands because they tend to ask too many questions, thus disrupting the service. I vaguely recall feeling a sense of injustice as I pondered why women needed to be kept in "time out" for something done so long ago in the early church.

Another memory also emerged, where my "injustice meter" was triggered by a sense of pain and disappointment. When no one else had stepped forward to serve as our church's Sunday school superintendent, an older, well-respected woman in our congregation volunteered. From my pew in the sanctuary where the junior high class sat together, I beamed with pride as Miss Flossie took the podium. She had been one of my favorite teachers—one of several men and women in our church who made a deep impact by reflecting Jesus to me. So it was a shock to my childish naivety when some of the men in the room stood up and walked out after Miss Flossie took the stage. One man appeared to mumble a disparaging comment, while the faces and body language of many others broadcasted their disapproval. As I sat across the room watching one of my mentors be rejected, I remotely felt the sting inflicted on her by gender-biases. In adulthood, I learned that many women have suffered a similar experience in various ministry settings.

Years after my wife's encounter with gender-exclusion, I faced another crossroad. Our first child came into our lives on a sunny October morning. As I gazed with wonder into my newborn daughter's eyes, I felt the weighty mantle of fatherhood descend. Tears filled my eyes, raw courage flooded my heart. With her tiny hand clutching my smallest finger, I spoke to my Bethany for the first time, making a solemn pledge: "I will do everything I can, by the grace of God, to see you become all that God made you to be. Every gift. Every dream. Every yearning of His heart for you fulfilled. Nothing holding you back. No tradition hindering you. No prejudice marginalizing you. I will fight for you." This promise was forged into my soul, and has gripped and motivated me ever since. I long to see that every man and woman—every son and daughter of God—has the freedom to pursue and fulfill his or her God-given destiny.

When I made that vow, I was oblivious to the commitment that would be required for the battle ahead. I had little awareness of the opposition I'd face, which has ranged from timeworn traditions to rigid mindsets to philosophies that appear to post "No Girls Allowed" placards on "Boys Only" clubhouses throughout our culture. As a father, this grieved me. Yet, the greatest shock of all came with the realization that the church has in many ways become one of the most stifling atmospheres for women. Daughters with ministry leadership callings upon their lives have struggled to respond to God's inner stirrings. They've felt conflicted in acknowledging their innermost dreams, as well as rebellious in beginning to pursue ministry pathways. As a pastor, this suppression grieved me.

I think it's only fair to share these experiences with you from the start, because they've impacted the course of my life. Let's face it—no one lives in a vacuum. All of us have faced both negative and positive incidents related to this issue. And we've drawn conclusions from our encounters, which grew into assumptions that affect us to this day. But, as I've studied biblical passages, examined theological deductions, and observed historical records, one conviction has guarded me: I don't want to allow my experiences to override sound exposition of the Scriptures. The following pages reflect my desire to honor that conviction.

Join me in an evaluation of where we've come from and where we're going. I promise that we won't throw stones at those who've gone before us, because we all walk in the light of our current understanding. Throughout this pursuit, I've had to grapple with my own obstacles—internal predispositions that labeled and marginalized my sisters, as well as interpretations of Scripture that seemed to sanctify these biases.

This expedition of mine has been filled with discovery. A huge part of the process has been pursuing and connecting with the heart of God. Sensing his yearning to see *all* of His children fully released to experience His dreams for them has overwhelmed me. As you consider the timeworn truths and fresh discoveries, pondering their impact on us personally and corporately, I encourage you to pursue the heart of God. Search the Scriptures and listen for His voice.

He is speaking.

And He is restoring everything we lost in Adam and Eve's revolt.

INTRODUCTION

There we sat—a huddled mass of 11-year-old boys sulking together on a bench at our community pool. With laser-like intensity, we glared at the three women in their rubber swimming caps covered with plastic daisies, floating and giggling in the hourly "Adult Swim." We sweltered as they swam. It was a mere ten-minute stint; but for us, it seemed like an eternity.

As we watched the final seconds tick away on the clock hung by the snack bar, we perched on the edge of the pool. Muscles straining, we awaited the lifeguard's whistle and the clarion cry: "Everybody in the pool!"

Splashes and cheers filled the air, as the barriers of exclusion were once again broken. I still smile when I recall those days.

No one likes feeling left out. From playground politics to high school hierarchies to boardroom blacklists—the hateful message gets perpetuated: "You are not wanted, nor are you needed." Countless daughters of God have received this message, and it has cut them to the core of their souls. It's caused them to compromise their callings, apologize for their opinions, and resign themselves to passive subordination.

Waves of people throughout human history have communicated this message in multifaceted ways. Ever since the fall in the Garden of Eden, the cruel "enmity" between the serpent and the woman has been released on the planet. Wherever darkness has prevailed, the lie of female inferiority has been imposed upon countless hearts.

But this is a new hour. Holy Spirit is brooding over the disorder, restoring broken relationships. The revival culture He's inspiring is surging with the atmosphere of heaven. It's as if the Lord of creation is blowing His whistle and declaring: "Everybody in the pool!" The freedom cry of multitudes of sons and daughters is being heard as we enter into all we have been created for—together!

CHAPTER 1

IN THE BEGINNING

"So God created humankind in his image, in the image of God he created them; male and female he created them."

Genesis 1:27 (NRSV)

The issue of women in ministry, especially women serving in church leadership, has been a hotly debated topic for generations. Diverse interpretations of scripture coupled with strong opinions have often drawn intense battle lines. In the words of Danny Silk, "The Bible is full of statements that can be, and have been, used to support two absolutely contradictory positions"[1] concerning women ministering and leading with men. Some have concluded that the Bible clearly presents a male-exclusive model for leadership, stating frankly, "God most often represents himself by male imagery. Christ became incarnate as a male. Hence, those who bring God's word, who speak for God in the assembly, should be men."[2] Others have come to the decision that ministry in the kingdom of God is filled with open opportunities for both genders, asserting, "The Scripture is clear. God's intent is for men and women to share as joint heirs, expressing together His grace and gifts to a wounded world."[3]

In such a divided climate, it's important for us to take a prayerful, thoughtful approach to interpreting key scriptures. Are the predominant male metaphors in the Bible used to describe God—as Father and King—proof that He's establishing a culture of male hierarchy? Does the sequential order of creation, God fashioning the man *before* the woman, also promote male supremacy? Does God create the most important member first, or does He save the best for last? Or, are *both* "very good" and equally precious in His sight? Are the instructions given in Paul's epistles concerning women specific advice to past situations, or are they permanent ecclesiastical commands? As we ponder these and other questions, let's start at the beginning. What is revealed in God's heart when the first man and woman were created?

GOD'S ORIGINAL INTENT

Let's take a look at Genesis 1:26-31, the Torah account of the formation of man and woman on the sixth day of creation. This short narrative captures God's original intent for the crown of His creation, male and female human beings made in His image. The care and honor taken in creating them, as well as the mantle of authority placed on them, is nothing short of amazing!

As we begin this study, it's important to share with you my personal convictions regarding biblical hermeneutics (i.e., the interpretation of scripture). First of all, I trust the accuracy of the original Old and New Testament texts. My approach in examining them is to discover God's revealed truth and its consistency with the comprehensive precepts of the Bible. Paul referred to the entirety of scripture as "the whole counsel of God,"[4] an encouragement for us to ask the question, "How does one passage align with the rest of the Bible?" Secondly, we need to understand each text in light of its historical and cultural setting. For example, Jesus citing how difficult it is for "a camel to go through the eye of a needle"[5] needs some background research and cultural context to discover its relevance for us today.

I approached this topic with sober awareness, realizing that, as a pastor, my explanation of scripture has a life-altering impact in multiple arenas. Not wanting my past experiences to jade my interpretation of the texts, I had to continually guard my heart, keeping it teachable before the Lord. And I had to face the fact that both my personal history and past religious instruction marginalized women from ministry involvement. I welcome you to join me in receiving this thoughtful challenge from author Fawn Parish: "We need to give each other time to unlearn habitual patterns of dishonor toward one another. We need to give grace, even as we challenge presuppositions."[6] With this resolve, let's take a look at Genesis.

GENESIS 1:26-31 (NIV)

Then God said, "Let us make mankind in our image, in our likeness, so that they may rule over the fish in the sea and the birds in the sky, over the livestock and all the wild animals, and over all the creatures that move along the ground." So God created mankind in his own image, in the image of God he created them; male and female he created them.

God blessed them and said to them, "Be fruitful and increase in number; fill the earth and subdue it. Rule over the fish in the sea and the birds in the sky and over every living creature that moves on the ground."

Then God said, "I give you every seed-bearing plant on the face of the whole earth and every tree that has fruit with seed in it. They will be yours for food. And to all the beasts of the earth and all the birds in the sky and all the creatures that move along the ground—everything that has the breath of life in it—I give every green plant for food." And it was so.

God saw all that he had made, and it was very good. And there was evening, and there was morning—the sixth day.

In this passage, we get a front row glimpse into the purposes of God for both men and women. Prior to this moment, everything was created by the voice of the Lord—from planets to puppies, and from oceans to guppies. All came into being by God's spoken word. The phrase "and God said" preceded every facet of creation's first five days. But the words, "Let us *make* mankind in our image," denote a shift to the intimate activity of God in the formation of the woman and the man. "Let us make" takes a "momentous step forward" in describing "God's personal involvement in the creation of humanity."[7]

If you would position your mouth a few inches from a pane of glass, then exhale onto it, allowing your warm breath to steam up the window—you'd see a physical accumulation of your DNA. The signature chemistry of who you are would be transferred to another object. This is what God did in creating us.

In the beginning, He fashioned us—male and female—from the soil of the earth. By breathing into this lump of clay, He conferred His very life to us, causing humanity to burst into existence. "A living being" emerged, filled with the DNA of God! How astonishing! We were made in the likeness of God, His handcrafted "masterpiece,"[8] as He breathed His very essence into us!

IN HIS IMAGE

"Let us make them in our image," was the initial creative declaration God made as the first humans were formed. Some have interpreted the plural "us" to represent a company of "heavenly beings who exist to do

God's bidding."[9] Those who hold to this view cite the early Hebrew belief that God frequently sought counsel from a host of angels.[10]

My personal understanding, however, agrees with those who see the "let us make" phrase as a reference to the Triune God—Father, Son, and Holy Spirit—expressing their wholehearted cooperation. Because God said, "Let us make humanity in *our* image," it's quite clear that we haven't been made in the image of angels. In fact, "no other biblical passage supports the idea that angels initiated the creation of human beings."[11] Instead, Scripture supports the corporate involvement of the Trinity throughout the creative process.

Elohim, the singular noun describing the only God, is used in the Hebrew text throughout Genesis 1 as the Triune Godhead works together as one. The Spirit of God appears at the beginning of the chapter, His hovering presence bringing order to chaos.[12] In John's Gospel, Jesus is referred to as the "Word," having active involvement in every facet of creation.[13] In fact, the plural "us" and "our" references to God in Genesis 1 "were regarded by the fathers and earliest theologians almost unanimously" to be "the Trinity."[14]

Ponder this thought with me: *Together* women and men mirror the image of God. One without the other results in a partial reflection of what God is like. Frank Gaebelein captures this amazing truth by stating: "As a grand mystery, the human relationship between man and woman reflects God's own personal relationship with Himself in three distinct persons we have come to call the Trinity."[15] Our shared origin shouts the fact that manifesting God's nature and ministering His heart will not happen apart from the collaboration of women and men!

Though both the man and the woman were fashioned in the likeness of God, some have interpreted his antecedence in creation as an indication of male supremacy. Those promoting this view believe that women should hold an inferior status. One such scholar sums up this thought by citing, "The fact that woman was derived from man," indicates "she was created to be subservient to man."[16]

Other explanations of the creation account have also been used to support this position. Some have referenced the phrase, "Let us make man (the Hebrew word *adam*) in our image"[17] as giving further support to a hierarchy of the genders. One researcher states, "God's naming the human race 'man' whispers male headship."[18]

Others continue this line of reasoning by highlighting that the responsibility to name the animals was given to the first man.[19] The ability to designate the identity of creatures is understood as the man exercising authority over them. Therefore, they say, when the man gives a name to the woman in Genesis 3:20, it's perceived that he's exercising authority over her, as well.[20]

My study has brought me to a different conclusion. I discovered that the Hebrew word *adam* is used in a broader sense, not exclusively referring to males. The Old Testament dialect "has no common term for humanity other than the word *adam*."[21] In fact, throughout the Old Testament, the word *adam* is used and is frequently translated as representing all human beings. Although it can be used as the proper name, "Adam," it's "most often a generic term for *both* male and female."[22] Therefore, the phrase "God created man" can best be translated as, "God created humanity in His image."

Since men and women have been created in the likeness of God, the reasonable conclusion is that God has both female and male attributes. God is not exclusively male nor female. Scripture reveals that God has compassion on us as a father,[23] yet God also gives nurturing care to us as a mother.[24] However, God is not a man or woman. God is Spirit, and we worship Him in spirit and in truth.[25] So, making God exclusively male is inconsistent with scripture. Insisting that God is male may have more to do with "reading our sexism into the biblical text," than allowing the Bible to speak for itself.[26] Because *both* men and women are made in the image of God, "women cease to be an appendix to the creation story."[27] We can feel the honor in God's voice as He speaks, "Let us create humanity in our image." His words flow without the slightest hint of "hierarchy, preference, superiority, or inferiority" toward either gender.[28] The human expression of the image of God would be incomplete if either gender were superior. Simply stated, "Both male and female are necessary," as equal partners reflecting the image of God.[29]

THE HELPER

Genesis 2 provides us with more information about the creation of the first man and woman. We learn that the woman is designed to be a "helper"[30] to the man. She is fashioned from the "rib" of the man.[31] And upon her creation, the man calls her "woman" for the first time.[32] These aspects of the creation of the woman have been seen by some as an indication of a male-superior hierarchy. Closer examination of the text, however, can support a different conclusion.

For many, the term "helper" can bring to mind examples of teams where one member is perceived to be a lesser sidekick. Think of Robin to Batman, Dr. Watson to Sherlock Holmes, or Ethel to Lucille Ball. When using these as a frame of reference, assigning the woman a role of "helper" relegates her to providing peripheral support with minimal input. However, other scriptural uses of the word "helper" reflect much more than a subservient function. In fact God, Himself, is frequently referred to as a "helper."[33] And in each of these passages it's never implied that God is inferior to those He's helping. Since God is never demeaned when He helps humans, a woman is not degraded when she's called a "helper."[34] Instead of seeing the word "helper" as the creation of a hierarchy, we can consider that God is bringing between men and women the relationship of dependency and reliability shared within the Godhead. Jesus' dependence on His Father[35] and His reliance on the Holy Spirit[36] reflect a healthy dynamic within their relationship.

Dependence on one another establishes an equality of purpose rather than relegation of status. In the same way, designating the woman to be a "helper" reveals her to be indispensable. The woman is essential to the man, but never inferior to him. Ultimately, as "helper" the woman is subordinate to the one who assigned her the responsibility to help. She's not subordinate to the man "with whom she is comparable," rather she's accountable to her Creator, to whom the man is also accountable.[37] To sum it up, as "helper," the woman is "a companion who is neither subordinate nor superior."[38] It seems consistent with both creation passages to see the creation of male and female as the establishing of a partnership rather than the creating of a hierarchy. Each partner compliments the other as they share in spiritual equality.

God also used the word "suitable" in reference to the woman. This means much more than finding Adam a wife who shares his interest in nature and enjoys long walks on the beach. "Suitable" speaks of one who is "identical in essence and substance; a social equal."[39] Putting these two words together, a "suitable helper" is far more than one who bakes muffins while Adam names animals. It speaks of the woman partnering with the man in fulfilling the purposes of God in the earth, sharing the same God-breathed essence, and uniting with him in fulfilling their divine destiny.

SIDE BY SIDE

Some have seen the statement in Gen. 2:22 as another picture of the woman's inferior role: "The rib that the Lord God had taken from the man He made into a woman." The deduction is that since she was fashioned second to the man and formed from a secondary part of the man—"merely a rib," her status must also be secondary. However, a closer examination of the term "rib" casts a different light on this verse.

The Hebrew word translated as "rib" (*tsela*) refers to "the side of the man, a part of the body that is neither above nor below him."[40] *Tsela* is an Old Testament Hebrew term used to describe the construction of the side of an object, such as the walls of the Tabernacle or the sides of the Ark of the Covenant."[41] It describes a crucial part of a structure, in no way designating a mere accessory. When God "made" the woman from the side of the man, the Hebrew verb *barah* is used, a term translated as "to build or creatively fashion a significant structure."[42] In light of this, the woman was carefully fashioned from a sizeable portion of the man and made into an essential creation in her own right.

In a similar way, the woman being formed from the side of the man *after* his creation doesn't make her secondary or of lesser value. The abbreviated creation account in Genesis 1:27 simply states, "Male and female he created them." The use of the word "them" indicates that God created the man and the woman as two human beings in their own right. This "completely overthrows the idea that man was at first androgynous" or asexual.[43] The woman was not a reduction of a genderless being. Rather she was fashioned as a uniquely valuable person, as was the man she was fashioned from. Although the man existed first, God made him unconscious, not giving him "a part in constructing the woman lest he be placed in a role as her creator."[44]

THE ORDER OF CREATION

The order of creation, namely the man being created before the woman, has also been interpreted as prioritizing his value. However, if the order of creation were a hierarchical indication of worth, then everything created before the man would supersede him. And if we reverse the process and view creation as progressively increasing in value, the woman would be seen as possessing greater significance than the man. The clearest contextual conclusion seems to be the thought that "the man and the woman were created sequentially in Genesis 2 in order to demonstrate their individual worth, as well as the need they have for each other."[45]

This is further underscored by the man's response to the woman when he sees her for the first time. Awakened from his God-induced sleep, he exclaims, "This is at last bone of my bones and flesh of my flesh!"[46] I have to admit that this somewhat strange exclamation can strike me as comical; it could have been delivered by a pirate of the Caribbean! However, I've come to appreciate the depth of the man's grateful astonishment. One author aptly describes this as "a cry of discovery and recognition as (the man) acknowledged her great value."[47] At the same time, he embraces the revelation that they share the same essential characteristics, namely "flesh of my flesh" and "bone of my bones." Because "flesh" frequently connotes weakness and "bone" represents strength, his words express a realization that "the man and the woman have both weaknesses and strengths as part of their shared humanity."[48] Rather than asserting that men and women are polar opposites (or from rival planets), Adam was affirming, "We have so much in common!"

NAME CALLING

The closing words of the man's joyful expression upon seeing the woman involve his declaration of her name. He announces, "She shall be called Woman, because she was taken out of Man!"[49] Some interpret his words as an affirmation of male supremacy in the male-female relationship. This statement by Thomas Schreiner typifies this premise: "When the man named the animals he exercised authority over them, and thus when he named the woman he exercised authority over her."[50] However, the mere act of naming the animals doesn't support the claim that he's taking authority over them. He is merely classifying them. Similarly, his statement to the woman is not his way of exercising authority over her. Instead, he's honorably recognizing the woman as one taken from him and corresponding to him in a divine compatibility.

His choice of names is tightly interconnected in the Hebrew language as he pronounces them "Man" *(ish)* and "Woman" *(ishah)*. These words are "so closely related that the only difference in their pronunciation is the feminine ending *ah*, meaning 'out from, yet together with.'"[51] Another rendering of the Woman's name could be "one who is equal; one who stands beside"[52] in a shared place of honor, authority, and destiny. As God completes this amazing creative process, we're told that He "blessed them,"[53] a picturesque term describing His wholehearted delight in them as He releases them to live in productive partnership.[54]

"LET THEM RULE!"

Following their creation, God made a profound pronouncement over the man and woman. He decreed: "Let them rule."[55] This wasn't a word spoken over Adam prior to the creation of Eve, calling the man to lead in solitude and the woman to follow in subservience. This was a manifesto pronounced over *both* of them, as *both* were called to lead together, serve together, and rule together on the earth. In God's image, they were created to manifest the same quality of interrelationship the Trinity thrives in—one filled with honor and respect, and wholly without jealousy or competition. Just as trust permeates the hearts of our Triune God, He made man and woman to entrust one another with their very lives. It's no wonder that immediately after creating them in His likeness, the Godhead exclaimed together, "This is *very* good!"

Prior to this joyous moment, God expressed a significant observation. Before fashioning the woman, He saw the man as isolated in a lush garden that was filled with plant and animal life, yet void of other human life. He decried, "It is not good for man to be alone."[56] This was much more than a desire on God's heart to find a wife for Adam. Instead it was a declaration of His longing to create the interdependent relationship between men and women—a relationship mirroring the unity and fellowship of the Godhead.

Sadly, this mutually honoring reflection of the image of God would soon be dissolved with the heartbreak of sin, deception, and division.

CHAPTER 2

DISHARMONY, DISUNITY, AND THE FALL OF HUMANITY

"The fall of man did not introduce evil; It placed us on the wrong side of it, under its rule, needing rescue."

—N. D. Wilson

Now the serpent was more crafty than any of the wild animals the Lord God had made. He said to the woman, "Did God really say, 'You must not eat from any tree in the garden'?" The woman said to the serpent, "We may eat fruit from the trees in the garden, but God did say, 'You must not eat fruit from the tree that is in the middle of the garden, and you must not touch it, or you will die.'" "You will not certainly die," the serpent said to the woman. "For God knows that when you eat from it your eyes will be opened, and you will be like God, knowing good and evil." When the woman saw that the fruit of the tree was good for food and pleasing to the eye, and also desirable for gaining wisdom, she took some and ate it. She also gave some to her husband, who was with her, and he ate it." Genesis 3:1-6 (NIV)

God fashioned us with great joy. Made in His likeness, we were created with an amazing capacity to experience His deep affections—knowing His love and sharing it with Him and one another. Paul's letter to the Ephesians captures this thought so well: *"Long before He laid down earth's foundations, He had us in mind, had settled on us as the focus of His love, to be made whole and holy by His love...What pleasure He took in planning this!"*[1]

Yet the exuberance of God in creation soon turned to deep grief, as the first man and woman rejected His clear command. They chose a self-driven pursuit of knowledge instead of a selfless dependence on Him. Blinded by the serpent's deception, they distanced themselves from God's life-giving presence. They chose independent information over interactive communication. Performance replaced intimacy. Driven-ness supplanted rest. Sadly, the once "very good"[2] human condition turned very bad.

This couple was created to rule in life together. They were made to experience and express the essence of God's glory—to live in harmony. God's intention was that His sons and daughters would be joint-heirs and co-laborers in non-hierarchical relationships. Both were endowed with power to make choices; hence both were honored as leaders in their own right. Their

Tree of the Knowledge of Good and Evil was given to the man *before* the woman's creation, when the serpent questioned her, the woman knew the command and recognized that it applied to her as well.[14] Some have suggested that Adam "did not faithfully pass the Word of the Lord on to Eve."[15] Yet Eve's response clearly shows that she was aware of both God's prohibition and the serious consequence of disobedience (i.e., *"You shall die."*). It's also important to note that the fall into sin was a joint decision. It wasn't simply the result of Adam's isolated neglect nor Eve's independent choice. Eve spoke for both of them as she took the fruit and said, *"We* may eat."[16]

SHARED RESPONSIBILITY

Some strongly believe that Eve is fully responsible for the decision to eat from the forbidden tree.[17] Yet the eating of the fruit seemed to happen almost simultaneously, as indicated by this statement: "She took of the fruit and ate; and she also gave some to her husband who was with her, and he ate."[18] This suggests that the man was a willing participant in the same temptation. Adam ate the fruit that was given to him without any hint of refusal or resistance.[19] This verse makes it clear that the man and the woman were "with" one another,[20] mutually involved in the process of hearing and yielding to the serpent's temptation. *"Both* participated in the choice to eat, *both* suffered the guilty results, for *both* knew it was forbidden."[21] Because God "created a system that allows for the power of human choice, humans have real power."[22] We are not merely puppets programmed to follow a formulated script. Since God held both the man and the woman accountable for their choices, both were treated equally as powerful individuals in their own right.

Following their disobedient choices, God addressed the man and the woman. It's noteworthy that He confronted them separately, thus affirming the authority each of them respectively carried.[23] He also spoke to them in the reverse order of their creation, approaching the woman first and then the man. This may seem like an insignificant point, but it's a Hebrew linguistic style that's common in Genesis. Known as a "concentric construction," it's used to dismantle any thought of a hierarchy.[24] Simply put, if Adam was predominant and Eve was subordinate, the man would consistently be addressed first.[25]

The couple's first response when confronted by God was to blame one another. Sin caused an immediate "loss of loving harmony between the man and the woman."[26] The shame they felt regarding their nakedness involved more than their sexuality. They abruptly realized "they had lost the divine glory which had once covered them."[27] Whereas they had previously been "naked and not ashamed,"[28] relating to one another in trusted vulnerability, their innocence was now "polluted with evil," and their transparency was infected with embarrassment and withdrawal.[29] Humiliated by their differences, they covered themselves from one another. What was once honored was now disgracefully concealed.

The situation was further complicated as they tried to hide themselves from God. Not only were their fig leaf coverings fruitless, their rebellious decisions resulted in relational ruin. Though aiming to be like God, they acted independently of Him—which ended in experiencing life outside of His best for them.[30]

GOD'S PAINFUL PRONOUNCEMENT

There in the Garden, God made one of the most pain-filled statements recorded in scripture. Finding the first couple huddled in a shroud of shame, He confronted them. Written like a song of lament, God pronounced the tragic results of their revolt. He described how their lives would be lived as a result of the Fall, vastly different from the life He had created for them. It's very clear that God is not describing "how their life should be lived."[31] He was neither ordaining nor approving these major alterations in their relationships. His words revealed a vicious torrent of distrust, discord, and domination that was foreign to the oneness of heart God had created them for—the quality of relationship God enjoyed within the Godhead. Adam and Eve were now experiencing the deadly results of which they had been warned. It wasn't the end of their physical life, but "separation from the possibility of free and perfect enjoyment of life by their separation from God, the Giver of life."[32]

God's first address to the woman in Genesis 3:16 concerned her joining with her husband to bear children. She would live up to her name, "Eve," reflecting her call to be "one giving and nurturing life."[33] Yet her childbirth experiences would be marked by pain. This would be a result of the disorder caused by sin "which disturbed the normal relation between [her] body and [her] soul."[34]

God's next pronouncement addressed the sin-altering change in the relationship between the man and the woman. He said to the woman, "Your desire will be for your husband, and he will rule over you."[35] Upon first glance, this can read as if it's a prescription to inflate the male ego (i.e., *I rule her—and she wants me!*). However, the desire God speaks of is not a sexual desire, but rather a "desire to dominate."[36] The same Hebrew word is used in Genesis 4:7 to describe sin's desire to "rule over" Cain. This term, describing "a violent craving for a thing,"[37] appears to be the woman's reaction to man ruling over her, and it illustrates a new posture—"a struggle of the wills between men and women."[38]

To best understand this scenario, we also need a clear explanation of the man's posture toward the woman. The term "rule over" speaks of "the man becoming a despotic ruler, crushing the woman as a slave."[39] The fruit of sin would include a man dominating a woman and a woman subordinating herself to a man in a way that was never intended in creation. Their mutual partnership would now be marred by resentment, domination, and disorder.[40]

How tragic! The woman, appointed to be the man's "equal beside" helper, would now resentfully struggle with his desire to demote her. Genesis 3:16 isn't a pronouncement for the man to "dominate the woman or for husbands to subjugate their wives."[41] Instead it was His sad commentary on the devastating culture of a sinful world. Far from God's joyful declaration upon the creation of the first man and woman, He now regrettably laments the brokenness caused by sin. He wasn't declaring life as it should be, but rather life as it would be under the curse of sin.

Both the man and the woman suffered great loss, as God expressed in their respective pronouncements. She would experience pain in childbirth.[42] He would encounter drudgery in his work.[43] In addition he would resentfully control her, and she would begrudge his fallen desire to dominate her. It's inaccurate to say the Genesis 3 account describes God's curse on women and men. In fact, He only cursed the serpent and the ground. Instead it illustrates one of the significant consequences of their rebellion. As Miguel De La Torre aptly states, "When the will of humans replaces God's will, all relationships are perverted."[44] He goes on to say, "The original relationship established by God in creation was replaced with the curse of patriarchal relationships" in which men seek absolute power over women.[45] Equality within the image of God was replaced by inequality within the image of fallen humanity. The once complimentary bond between men and women "has now been distorted and damaged by sin."[46] Women will struggle with a sinful desire to oppose men, and men will have a distorted aspiration to dominate women. "One of the most tragic results of sin is this ongoing conflict between men and women."[47] The struggle for domination over one another is not presented here as an ideal, but rather as the sad reality of human history. Like the thorns and thistles springing up from the ground, this was a grievous departure from the initial glory of creation.

Yet even in His verdict, God gives a glimpse of future redemption in Genesis 3:15. This resilient hope lies in His pronouncement that a "seed" will arise to strike the head of the serpent and overcome the effects of his devious temptation and humanity's rebellious fall. Through the centuries, most biblical scholars have concluded that this "seed" points to "one solitary person" empowered to restore what was forfeited.[48] Clearly, this seed is Jesus, the fulfillment of multiple Old Testament prophecies, including God's prophetic declaration in the shadow of the Fall. Jesus would come to restore everything that was lost in the rebellion![49]

CHAPTER 3

OLD TESTAMENT GLIMPSES OF THE RESTORATION OF GOD'S ORIGINAL INTENT

"Women were created from the rib of man to be beside him, not from his head to top him, nor from his feet to be trampled by him, but from under his arm to be protected by him, near to his heart to be loved by him, by his side to rule with him."

—Matthew Henry,
An Exposition of the
Old and New Testament

"It is very clear that the 'dominion' was never intended to be man's dominion over woman. But as "them"—together sharing in a mutually honoring role of authority over all things."

—Dake's Bible,
study notes on Gen. 1:26

Centuries would pass before Jesus, the promised "seed," would come to restore the relationship between humanity and God, as well as the bond between women and men. In spite of the fact that restoration was awaiting Messiah's arrival, some of our Jewish fathers and mothers modeled a mutually honoring camaraderie as they served the purposes of God together. They rose to places of influence and obedience to God's call on their lives amid a climate of resistance.

WOMEN'S WORLD IN POST-FALL ISRAEL

In Old Testament times, the effect of sin and its aftermath were freshly felt. The harsh enmity between Satan and the woman was evident, and often cruelly acted out in society. "Women were often viewed and treated as possessions—as 'less than men.'"[1] Strewn throughout the historical accounts of scripture are stories of terrible abuse and violence toward women. From Sarah's harsh mistreatment of her servant, Hagar,[2] to Lot's willingness to callously surrender his daughters to a violent mob,[3] to the graphic abuse of a young woman in Judges 19—life for women in the Old Testament culture was far from easy. Even so some women learned to rise above the culture in response to God's call on their lives. "When a woman was the right person for the job," states Ruth Haley Barton, "God didn't hesitate to use her. And the results were impressive."[4]

Miriam, Moses' and Aaron's sister, was recognized as a prophet by both her brothers as well as by the children of Israel.[5] Years later the prophet Micah affirmed Miriam's role as a leader among God's people.[6] Huldah, a woman clearly called and confirmed as a prophet, was consulted for wisdom by both the king and the high priest.[7] In fact the prophet Isaiah's wife was also recognized as a prophet in her own right.[8] Hebrews 11 cites Sarah as a significant woman of influence whose faith, along with her husband Abraham's trust in God, created the nation of Israel and forged God's covenant with His people. We could go on to mention Queen Esther and Ruth and other lesser-known women who played important parts in the purpose of God for His people, ultimately impacting all nations and future generations. Each of these women made substantial contributions as leaders in their own rite.

OLD COVENANT COMRADERIES

Perhaps the clearest example of male/female collaboration in leadership is recorded in Judges 4 and 5. Deborah and her male counterpart, Barak, profoundly impacted history as a team of deliverers, or "judges," releasing Israel from 20 years of oppression under Jabin, the king of the Canaanites. Unlike Abraham and Sarah, Deborah and Barak were not a married couple. Both had loyal spouses of their own. Neither one "married into the ministry." They served in their ministry roles because of their individual callings, not their spousal connection.

Deborah assumed a variety of leadership roles. She served Israel as a prophet,[9] as a judge,[10] and as a "mother of Israel."[11] In her judicial role, Deborah handled some of the most difficult cases under a palm tree in the hill country of Ephraim, a location dedicated for the more serious disputes.[12] In her honor the site was named "the palm of Deborah,"[13] and the title "mother of Israel" was bestowed on her. The phrase "in Israel" recognizes her as an influential national leader.[14] "Mother in Israel" could be "comparable today to an honorary doctorate bestowed in recognition of national leadership contributions."[15] She could have been a "stand alone" leader in her own rite. It makes her even more prestigious when noting that she chose to "stand beside" Barak in a shared leadership role.

From her position of authority, Deborah used her influence and favor to call Barak into his destiny.[16] In turn Barak said to her, "If you go with me, I will go; but if you don't go with me, I won't go."[17] Barak's statement could be paraphrased like this: *"Just as you called me into my destiny as a warrior, so I am linking my destiny to yours! I call you into your destiny as a strategic leader who hears from God. Our gifts are incomplete without each other. Therefore, I am not going without you!"* Barak's words clearly express the heart of God for His sons and daughters to serve and lead together!

Deborah then encouraged Barak to conquer General Sisera, the commander of the Canaanite army, prophetically declaring his imminent victory.[18] The mutually honoring atmosphere permeating this partnership so reflects the image of God. The camaraderie pervading the joint activity of the Godhead in creation was manifested on the earth as Deborah and Barak overcame Israel's enemies together. After Sisera's defeat, Deborah and Barak joined their voices in singing a victory song. The first stanza of their anthem is quite insightful. They sang: *"When the princes of Israel take the lead, when the people willingly offer themselves—praise the Lord!"*[19] Take note of the reference to "princes"—multiple leaders acknowledging their place of royal influence—taking the lead together! This side-by-side collaboration of Barak and Deborah generated a spirit of unity and spontaneous devotion among the people. When sinful competition gives way to supernatural cooperation, refreshing waves of unity are released throughout the corporate body! The people also *"willingly offer themselves."*

Some have said that the women of Israel led when there was a shortage of male leadership, implying that God made rare exceptions in the absence of gifted men. However biblical history does not support that theory. Deborah was clearly gifted and called by God to lead, comfortably serving beside Barak. And Barak's military leadership gifts only enhanced and supported Deborah's apt headship. It's quite significant that Barak refused to lead in the military crisis without Deborah by his side!

The prophet Huldah gave strong leadership to the nation at a time when there was no scarcity of gifted men. She ministered in the same era as Nahum, Habakkuk, Jeremiah, and Zephaniah, who were also in their prophetic prime.[20] When King Josiah charged his advisors to seek counsel regarding a difficult decision, His male advisors went directly to Huldah.[21] They had a wide array of male prophets to choose from, but Huldah was their prophet of choice.

We must face the fact that throughout Old Testament accounts, there are more men than women in leadership positions. However, it would be inaccurate to conclude that this resulted from women being less gifted or unsuited for leadership responsibilities. It would be equally unfair to surmise that the instances of female leadership recorded in the Old Testament were inappropriate. Although women were excluded from the Levitical priesthood, biblical records document women and men serving together in many other roles. "There is every indication that women and men worshiped and ministered side by side."[22] Both men and women were involved in building the tabernacle.[23] They also shared the responsibility of guarding the entrance to the tabernacle.[24] Women and men jointly led the people during national feast days and public processions,[25] playing instruments, dancing, singing together in the choirs, and offering sacrifices.[26]

"Scripture makes it clear that humanity's fundamental problem is sin—rebellion against the Creator—not male oppression."[27] Men were not the enemies. The serpent was the enemy, and temptation was his weapon—part of his ultimate scheme to divide and conquer. Unity between these men and women served to frustrate the enemy's plans, while simultaneously fulfilling the purposes of God. As godly sisters served beside their brothers, their incentive was to support the ministry, not to supplant the men. Though sin had clearly scarred the relationship between the genders, Old Testament history attests to brave women and courageous men who refused to be sidelined by the iniquities of their Eden parents.

A NEW DAY DAWNING

The prophet Joel, among the final prophetic voices of the Old Testament era, spoke of an amazing new day when Heaven would invade earth in restorative splendor. The Holy Spirit would be poured out upon all people, culminating in supernatural wonders and an abundant spiritual harvest. A critical component in this outpouring would be the uniting of sons and daughters as one prophetic voice. All ages and both genders would play keys roles in this coming move of God on the earth. The deadly breach between sons and daughters would be reversed. The Lord's heart for His children is captured in this phrase: *"Even on my servants, both men and women, I will pour out my Spirit in those days."*[28] Both sons and daughters would experience the Father's outpouring of intimacy and power. No one would be excluded! Within a few centuries, this prophecy would begin to be fulfilled with the arrival of Jesus, the Messiah. But even as this word was being spoken, dark forces were inciting the emerging Roman Empire to wage another war on the women and men of Israel, causing further pain and division.

CHAPTER 4

THE HIGH COST OF COMPROMISE

"Don't you know that when you allow even a little lie into your heart, it can permeate your entire belief system?"

Galatians 5:9 (TPT)

OF ROMANS AND RABBIS

Despite Israel's legacy of godly men and women working together, the invasion of the Roman Empire served to dissipate their rich heritage. Some Jews succumbed to the values of their pagan neighbors, adopting Roman ways as their own. While others, led by the rabbis, observed stricter laws in an attempt to defend Jewish culture from the Graeco-Roman way of life. These teachings of the rabbis, contained in the Tosefta, the Jerusalem Talmud, and the Babylonian Talmud, were added to the Word of God as a protective shield against Roman culture.[1]

Though Roman males did not treat women as their equals, women were not completely marginalized in Roman society. The general attitude toward their female counterparts could be summarized as indifferent. One historian notes, "Perhaps the ambivalent attitude of Roman men to their women is best summarized by the words of Metellus Numidicus who was quoted in a speech by Augustus when the emperor addressed the assembly, 'Nature has made it so that we cannot live with them [women] particularly comfortably, but we can't live without them at all.'"[2]

The rabbis, however, did not respond to Roman indifference toward women with an opposing liberating view. The rabbinical rules that impacted New Testament culture were predominantly gender-biased, as well. Reflected throughout the rabbis' writings is a predominant spirit of male superiority. One not so subtle text states, "Compared with Adam, Eve was like a monkey to a human being."[3] Similar to the Greek myth blaming the goddess Pandora for all of the world's evils, these rabbinical teachings placed the full blame for the fall at the feet of Eve and, by implication, on the shoulders of all women. As one writing summarized: "Woman is more prone to sin than man."[4] Yet another vilified all women, stating, "Woman was the beginning of evil."[5]

The status of married women, according to these documents, was far from the image of the co-reigning partners of Genesis. Many rabbinical laws classified wives together with cattle, real estate, and other possessions.[6] In New Testament times, it was relatively easy for a husband to divorce, or "discard," his wife. In a moment of decreased attraction to her or increased frustration with her, a husband could terminate his marriage by writing and signing a simple document. At the same time, it was virtually impossible for a woman to divorce her husband, even when the relationship had become abusive. One rabbi summarized this degraded view of wives by stating: "Whereas an owner can give up his property, property cannot abandon its owner."[7]

This gender hierarchy was not only felt in the home, it carried over into the corporate worship life of the Jewish community. Hebrew women were not allowed to participate in the most important annual rituals. They were also confined to a segregated portico in Herod's temple, "even though this was not part of God's original design for the tabernacle...nor in Solomon's temple."[8] Women were also forbidden to read the Torah, both for private study and for public services. As one rabbi avowed, "The reading of the Torah by a woman would dishonor the community."[9] In addition most rabbis refused to teach the Torah to a woman, viewing her as incapable of learning the Law of Moses. One rabbi went so far as to refer to a woman as an "ignoramus" when attempting to comprehend spiritual matters.[10]

Whether by Roman intusion or rabbinical exclusion, women in Israel during this chapter in history keenly experienced marginalization. The cultural climate was highly oppressive. Not only were women forbidden to speak in the synagogues and restricted to only the "outer court" areas of the temple, they were not even allowed to speak openly with men in public! While a wife could converse quietly in public with her husband, that was only if he gave her permission to do so. Adding further humiliation, women were never called to testify in court. The reason? Their testimony was considered unreliable, based on a stereotype of women as predominantly emotional and minimally factual. These and other practices sent a clear message to women that they had little or no value.

THE NEED FOR THE SEED

All of this occurred in a roughly 400-year period between the days of prophet Malachi and the arrival of Messiah Jesus. In that relatively brief time, a strong gender hierarchy was solidified. The vicious cycle of male domination and female frustration seemed as if it would never disappear from the planet. Yet into this climate, Jesus, the foretold Seed, became flesh and lived among us.

Knowing this cultural backdrop to His arrival is enlightening. Seeing His responses to the social mores is even more revealing. Jesus came to tear down every stronghold that opposed His Father's will. He came to establish a new Kingdom order, no longer reminiscent of the Fall. It would be reflective of Heaven. While His ways were offensive to many, His interactions were liberating and His transformations were radical. Not everyone understood Him. Many opposed Him. Yet the impact of His arrival would prove to be the most revolutionary period in human history!

CHAPTER 5

JESUS THE REVOLUTIONARY RESTORER

"If we are to better the future—we must disturb the present."
—Catherine Booth

What Jesus said and did, in light of the climate of His day, revealed His compassionate and revolutionary heart. He neither catered to cultural biases nor bowed to rabbinical dogma. Instead He allowed people to experience the liberating atmosphere of His Kingdom. By His teaching and actions, Jesus clearly communicated the heart of His Father toward both men and women. He acknowledged their common origin and joint destiny. He empathized with them in their shared tragedy, the results of Eden's revolt. Yet He inspired them to hope for an increasing partnership, both with Him and with one another, in the restoration of His Kingdom on the earth.

JESUS' KINGDOM CULTURE CLASH

At a time when women had limited access to key sacred spaces in edifices of worship and instruction,

Jesus intentionally avoided those exclusionary places. Women were banned from most of Herod's temple, relegated only to the outer court of the building. Hence Jesus taught in the "Solomon's Portico" section of the temple,[1] the only area accessible to both women and men. In addition, Jesus frequently taught in open public places where both genders and all ages could partake. He clearly came to tear down dividing walls and demolish biased barriers.

In light of the fact that women were forbidden by rabbinical law to speak with men in public, Jesus' pattern of having open conversations with women in open places was shocking. Jesus frequently healed and interacted with both men and women in public settings, demonstrating the same compassion and honoring dialogue toward all. Amazingly, Jesus' lengthiest recorded interaction with an individual took place with a Samaritan woman beside the town well (John 4:7-26). She had been rejected by five husbands, was labeled and shunned by many of her neighbors, and had arrived at the well to draw water at an unusual time of day, presumably to avoid further painful interactions with people. Yet Jesus connected with and ministered to her without hesitation. When Jesus' disciples returned from searching for food, they seemed indignant that Jesus had "wasted" an afternoon talking with a woman. Much to their chagrin, Jesus highlighted this conversation with the Samaritan woman as a vital part of His ministry. He refused to be hindered by stifling edicts that were contrary to His value system. Jesus unabashedly honored women.

To further confirm His esteemed view of women, Jesus not only talked with women, He also taught them. Most rabbis viewed women as incapable of learning and unworthy of the time invested in attempting to teach them. Statements throughout the Jerusalem Talmud reinforced this opinion, such as: "Let the words of *Torah* be burned up, but let them not be delivered to women."[2] Jesus openly defied this sentiment. Most notably, Rabbi Jesus taught Mary, the sister of Martha and Lazarus, as she sat at his feet.[3] This detail is noted in Luke's Gospel because sitting at the feet of a rabbi was the formal mentoring posture of rabbinical instruction. The apostle Paul would later cite the fact that he had been formally instructed at the feet of his rabbi, Gamaliel.[4] Jesus' closest followers were called "disciples," a term commonly used to describe the formal students of a rabbi. With this in mind, it's insightful to note that approximately half of Jesus' closest followers were women, a number of whom supported His ministry financially.[5] Although Jesus' constant companions were a group of men often referenced as "The Twelve," these men were not His only disciples. Both women and men were taught rabbinically by Jesus in His co-ed Kingdom training school.

The male-exclusive Pharisees and other religious leaders in New Testament times enjoyed public notoriety. On several occasions Jesus pointed out their love for the praise of men. He noted their regular habit of praying loudly in congested areas in order to be both seen and presumed to be spiritual.[6] They also delighted in bringing their offerings to the temple amid much fanfare, at times accompanied by a musical entourage announcing their grandiose donations. On one such occasion, as wealthy men gave boisterously, Jesus noted a widow who quietly gave a small yet sacrificial gift as her offering. Jesus honored this woman's generous heart as she silently gave all she had to please God, in sharp contrast to the flamboyant male donors who gave to please men. Jesus honored this woman because of what He saw in her heart. In the same way, He honored the trusting hearts of a number of women who were His followers. On several occasions He referred to them as "daughters of Abraham."[7] Shockingly, this phrase was uncommon in Hebrew culture. While men were frequently referred to as "sons of Abraham," women were virtually never referenced in light of their spiritual heritage. Jesus began a new, restorative trend of openly honoring both women and men for their internal qualities. He was asserting that in His Kingdom, honor will be the ambiance—for both men and women.

In the culture of Jesus' day, dishonoring women had one of its greatest expressions in the distrust of women. In the rabbinical school of thought, women bore the primary responsibility for the fall from grace in Eden. And in the event of an adulterous relationship, women were commonly thought to be the ultimate perpetrators of the infidelity. Women were generally viewed as fickle and unreliable, and therefore couldn't testify in a court of law, as their recollection of events was deemed untrustworthy. Knowing that this prevalent mindset existed makes it astonishing that Jesus' entrusted several women with the testimony of His resurrection. At a time when women couldn't appear in court, Jesus gave the women who discovered His empty tomb the awesome responsibility of telling His male disciples that He was indeed alive. In fact when Jesus learned that His male disciples had rejected the credibility of the women's report, He soundly rebuked them for their distrust and dishonor.[8] Jesus made it clear that he wouldn't allow marginalizing traditions to keep both His sons *and* His daughters from having full participation and equal inheritance in His Kingdom.

As Jesus prepared His first-generation followers for His final days on earth and their strategic mission, His simple instructions were insightful. Water baptism became the new, binding sign of the new covenant. No longer would circumcision, a male-exclusive event, be the indication of covenant. An external mark was replaced by an internal work—something open and accessible to both daughters and sons. Additionally, the outpouring of the Holy Spirit would be upon both men and women. Daughters and sons would be filled and would prophesy, literally being saturated by and bubbling forth with fresh revelation of the heart of God. In short, Jesus said that men and women will receive, men and women will be empowered, and men and women will partner together in this amazing move of God upon the earth!

CHAPTER 6

PIONEERING PARTNERSHIPS

"If you want to go fast, go alone. If you want to go far, go together."

—African proverb

For many years I saw the New Testament account of the early church as a testimony to a predominantly male-led movement of first-generation believers. Jesus passed the baton to the eleven remaining *male* disciples. The Gospels were written by four *male* eyewitnesses to His ministry. The epistles, as well, were authored by apostolic *men* giving instruction, correction, and direction to this emerging company of Jesus-followers. Yet upon closer examination, I discovered powerful examples of pioneering partnerships of men *and* women working together to advance the Kingdom.

THEY WERE TOGETHER

From the earliest days of the church, *both* men *and* women gathered in the upper room to pray and wait for the outpouring of the Holy Spirit. The 120 individuals assembled that day were identified as those who had followed Jesus from the beginning of His ministry.[1] New Testament records clearly account for *both* male and female disciples accompanying Jesus on His earliest ministry trips.[2] Included in the Pentecost congregation were Mary Magdalene, Joanna, and Mary, James' mother.[3] Additionally the mother of the sons of Zebedee was in attendance.[4] Still others, namely Joses and Salome, plus Mary, the wife of Peter, were recognized among this company of devoted followers.[5] Although we don't have a roster of everyone present that day, we shouldn't assume that those among the remaining 120 were all male disciples.

Those days of passionate anticipation for the awaited deluge of the Spirit were most likely filled with lots of interaction. Relationships had been strained during the previous days surrounding the crucifixion of Jesus. The male disciples had dispersed in fear when He was arrested.[6] Peter had accused the rest of the disciples of cowardice, proudly stating that he would never abandon Jesus in the face of fierce opposition by the religious leaders.[7] Then, ironically, Peter denied any affiliation with Jesus when questioned.[8] Several women, along with John, appeared to be among a small remnant who stood by the cross as Jesus died.[9] These same women were the first to discover His empty tomb several days later. However, the male disciples refused to believe the women's report—a decision Jesus would later soundly rebuke them for.[10] The level of tension in that upper room may have been at an all-time high.

But when the day of Pentecost came, these 120 individuals were gathered in one heart and mind, indicating that significant reconciliation had occurred.[11] Serious prayer and honest dialogue between both men and women most definitely contributed to this. And the response of these 120 believers to the sudden influx of 3,000 new Jesus-followers reflects wisdom and solidarity.[12] The fact that they relatively quickly assimilated several thousand people into fellowship groups, discipling clusters, and benevolence ministries indicates administrative savvy.[13] So it's no stretch for me to believe that *both* women and men were part of the upper room discernment and decision-making process.

PAUL AND WOMEN

The apostle Paul encountered women in church leadership long before he became a follower of Jesus. Commissioned to shut down the church, Paul (then Saul) arrested *both* men and women believers. He *"ravaged the church, entering house after house, dragging off both men and women and delivering them to prison."*[14] In fact *both* women and men were seen as such a threat that the High Priest and the governing Council licensed Paul to arrest and imprison Christian men and women, tracking them to regions far beyond Jerusalem.[15] In the eyes of the religious authorities, the early church "included women who were just as dangerous in their heresy as the men, and Paul treated them alike."[16]

Paul's high estimation of women as leaders, from his days of persecuting the church, continued after he received Jesus and became a builder of the church. On one of his earliest missionary journeys to Europe, Paul, accompanied by Luke and Silas, arrived at the city of Philippi. There they met a group of women gathered by a riverbank and began telling them about Jesus. Paul's first convert in Europe was a woman named Lydia, whom he personally baptized.[17] Lydia grew spiritually, eventually becoming a dynamic influence in the church at Philippi.

Lydia was a businesswoman, manufacturing purple cloth. Her successful enterprise and her quality product made her quite influential in that region. The fact that Luke mentions her by name in Acts 16 reflects her valued role, both in the business world as well as the church world. Paul and his team spent several weeks investing time ministering to Lydia. Luke records the fact that "the Lord opened Lydia's heart,"[18] indicating her receptivity to the theological and pastoral training she would receive from Paul. It appears very likely that he was equipping her to care for the church after he would travel to minister in other parts of Macedonia. Because Lydia is the only Philippian convert mentioned by name, and because the Philippian church met in her home, she would be the most likely person to have led and cared for the first congregation at Philippi. Lydia, like other women of her day, was not marginalized from ministry. Her open heart and open home provided a place for the Philippian church to grow and influence their world.

Paul's ministry was continually directed toward both women and men. Wherever he preached, both genders responded to his message.[19] Both male and female believers were frequently mentioned by name, reflecting their shared importance in advancing the church. In Athens, after a sizeable number of men and women responded to the gospel, two individuals are mentioned by name. Luke records a man named Dionysius and a woman named Damaris[20] as being included among these new converts. Mentioning them by name often indicates their recognition by others as being leaders of influence within their culture.

Paul's letters also reflect his value of both male and female leaders among the churches. Years after leaving Philippi, he wrote to the congregation. Among his words of instruction and encouragement, he included a corrective word to two female leaders, Euodia and Syntyche, asking them to resolve their conflict. Taking the time to mention this in a corporate letter indicates their place of influence in the church. He references them as leaders "who contended at my side in the cause of the gospel, along with Clement and the rest of my co-workers."[21]

In his letter to the Corinthian church, Paul acknowledges Prisca (Priscilla) and Aquila, a married leadership team whose home was the gathering place for the emerging church in Corinth.[22] Paul, on several occasions, cherished his opportunities to minister side by side with this couple.[23] In a subsequent letter Paul honored both Prisca and Aquila as his "fellow workers in Christ Jesus."[24] He credits them as leaders who "risked their lives for me." He further states, "Not only I but all the churches of the Gentiles are grateful for them."[25]

In the final words of his letter to the Romans, Paul honors a number of church leaders by name, acknowledging their vital contributions to the spread of the Gospel. Twenty-six people are noted, ten of whom are women. The first person on his list is Phoebe, a deacon of the church in Cenchrea.[26] Paul refers to her as a leader who "has been a great help to many people, including me."[27]

Her role as "deacon" has been translated by some as "deaconess." However, the same masculine form of the word "deacon" is used both in the Roman passage as well as throughout the rest of the New Testament. Hence the role of a "deacon," one who serves as servant-leader in various ministry responsibilities of the church, was one held by *both* women and men. The term "deacon" has also been translated as "minister," because it includes the ministries of teaching and preaching. The same term is used to describe the ministries of Paul, Barnabas, and Apollos.[28] Phoebe, a minister from the church in Cenchrea, was sent by that church to Rome on a special ministry assignment, and Paul honored her for her vital role.

Another leader mentioned on the Romans 16 list is a woman named Junia, referred to as someone serving in the office of an apostle. Paul writes, "Greet Andronicus and Junia, my relatives, who have been in prison with me. They are outstanding among the apostles, and they were in Christ before I was."[29] Andronicus is a masculine name. Junia is a feminine name. However, some have attempted to translate her name as "Junias," a masculine name. This significant alteration is not supported by several key factors.

Primarily, all Greek New Testament manuscripts contain the feminine form of "Junia," not the male name "Junias." Additionally, the female name Junia was very common during that time period, while the male name, Junias, is uncommon to that era. Finally, Junia was "universally recognized as a female apostle for the first several centuries of Church history."[30] The fifth century church father, John Chrysostom, wrote regarding Junia, "Oh how great is the devotion of this woman, that she should be even counted worthy of the appellation of apostle."[31]

In other letters Paul acknowledged Chloe[32] and Nympha[33] as two women to be honored for their leadership roles in the church. Paul doesn't appear to have any reluctance in respecting leadership gifts and callings in either gender. This is further supported in his letters to young pastor Timothy. In his instructions to his spiritual son, Paul encouraged Timothy to take all that he had learned and "pass [it] on to faithful leaders who are competent to teach congregations the same revelation."[34] Many versions of this verse interpret it to say, "Entrust [what I have taught you] to faithful *men*," supporting a male-only succession in leadership training. However, Paul didn't use the term "andros" in this statement, which would have referred to only men. Instead Paul used the term, "anthropoi," which refers to *both* men and women.[35] A faithful rendering of this verse could be, "Entrust what I have taught you to loyal men and women who will, in turn, train other men and women."

According to Paul's missionary trips and apostolic letters, men and women served side by side in ministry partnerships in the first-generation church. The Book of Acts and Paul's epistles reflect women serving as apostles, prophets, teachers, deacons, ministers, church-planters, and pastors.[36] Paul honors men and women elders as spiritual fathers and mothers in the church family.[37] In his letter to Titus, Paul entreats women elders to behave in a way befitting those called to "priestly leadership."[38] It should be noted that these women are not being addressed because they're advanced in age. They are "elder" women, serving in leadership roles with "elder" men, giving collaborative oversight to the church. Paul also recognizes women as part of pastoral teams overseeing house churches.[39] In the same spirit, John honors an unnamed woman in his second epistle, calling her a "chosen lady," a term often used to describe an elder, overseer, or pastor.[40]

Women such as Lydia, Phoebe, Junia, Prisca, Chloe, and Nympha were not marginalized in the early years of the church. They were bold in evangelism, compassionate in pastoring, wise in oversight, and unflinching under persecution. They cared for people and were strategic leaders on the frontlines of the advancing church, spurred on by Paul's bold assertion that every member had a vital place of ministry in Jesus' body.

CHAPTER 7

DECLARATION OF INTERDEPENDENCE

"For though we are many, we've all been mingled into one body in Christ. This means that we are all vitally joined to one another, with each contributing to the others."
Romans 12:5 (TPT)

Paul's letter to the Galatian church is one of the saddest commentaries on how subtly we can slip from liberty to legalism. Abandoning self-denial and joyful dependence on Jesus, these early believers descended into self-righteous independence. Where they were once making great progress spiritually, joyfully running their race, they were now hindered by lifeless, loveless religion.[1] It impaired their view of God, and it impacted their relationships with one another. Rather than building one another up, they began to tear one another down with harsh judgmentalism. One translation describes their behavior this way: *"You continue to criticize and come against one another over minor issues. You're acting like wild beasts trying to destroy one another."* [2]

Paul understood this behavior all too well. As a Pharisee he had prided himself in his ability to keep the letter of the Law. Calling himself a "Pharisee of the Pharisees,"[3] he viewed his own performance as superior to other religious leaders who were also aspiring for perfection. While publicly respected, he was inwardly tormented by his own hypocrisy and failure.[4] Grateful to be set free from such religious torment by the grace of Jesus, he was grieved to see these Galatian believers falling into similar bondage.

GALATIAN SEGREGATION

This crisis began when Jewish Christian extremists infiltrated the Galatian church. Losing sight of all Jesus had accomplished by His death and resurrection, these dogmatic teachers demanded strict adherence to ceremonial laws in order to earn right-standing with God. They insisted that all Gentile men be circumcised. In addition, they imposed harsh dietary stipulations and enforced rigorous Sabbath laws. The results were tragic. The Galatians' rest in their acceptance in Christ and delight in His gift of righteousness were disrupted by this wave of religious striving. Their revelation of a new oneness shared by all who are in Christ was replaced by a divisive caste system. Fault lines of ethnicity, social status, and gender emerged, with separation growing and becoming the norm.

Paul responds by addressing the issues at their roots. He begins by reiterating the purpose of the Law before it was turned into the legalistic agenda of these infiltrators. He describes the Mosaic Law as a "disciplinarian," also referred to as a "pedagogue."[5] Common in Greco-Roman homes, the pedagogues were trusted servants responsible for supervising the moral behavior of the sons in the family.[6] The pedagogue's main duty was to make sure each boy followed the household laws, serving as their constant conscience.[7] This role continued until the sons reached manhood.

Paul describes "life under the Law" as one of perpetual immaturity, in need of persistent prompting.[8] The Law's purpose is to "impede us" by "holding us in conviction of sin," while being in itself powerless to change us.[9] Through the Law we're made aware of God's standards, our own weakness, and our desperate need of a Savior. Therefore Paul says the Law's function in God's plan is limited, until we receive Jesus and are justified by faith in Him.[10] Our new standing with God is no longer based on "law observance, but on faith."[11] Under the Law we endured "an immature life of slavery under the guardian."[12] Now, as spiritual sons and daughters, we share in the family inheritance and have a voice in the family authority.[13] In a very real sense, the "let them rule" commission conferred upon the man and the woman in the Garden,[14] and lost in the Fall has now been fully restored in Jesus.

Paul's statement, "For in Christ you are all children of God through faith,"[15] is a life-altering declaration. The word "children," translated by some as "sons,"[16] is a "legal term used in the adoption laws of first-century Rome" and describes sons *and* daughters who fully enjoy "all the privileges, responsibilities, and inheritance rights of natural children."[17] In fact Gentile and Jewish believers in Jesus are given "even higher status than being the 'sons of Abraham,' they are now sons of God in Christ Jesus.'"[18] According to Paul, this transition into the supernatural life of Jesus is the ultimate transformation of our personal world, as well as our corporate world! In response to the legalistic infiltrators, Paul boldly states: "Circumcision doesn't mean a thing to me. The only thing that really matters is living by the transforming power of this wonderful new creation life.'"[19]

Paul uses two powerful phrases to describe how radical our new life in Jesus really is. First he states that we "were baptized into Christ."[20] The root meaning of the word "baptized" carries the thought of being so immersed, we "absorb the qualities of the immersing substance and thus are transformed."[21] In such an absorbed relationship with Jesus, we're literally "incorporated into Him."[22] The preposition "into," used in the phrase "baptized *into* Christ," is a more powerful word than the preposition "in." "Into" speaks of "a radical immersion resulting in a dramatic transformation in which Christ is fully revealed and fully received."[23] This quality of relationship was impossible under the Law. This radically new nearness cannot be achieved by human effort, but becomes our new reality by faith in Jesus.

Paul's second word picture of this unprecedented connection with Jesus is captured in the phrase, "[You] have clothed yourselves with Christ."[24] The concept of putting on a new person implies an entirely new way of life, a new spiritual and social status, and "an entirely new order of existence."[25] In a very real sense, stripped of their old identity, these Galatian believers had acquired a "new identity that lies beyond all ethnic, social, and sexual distinctions. In a word, the Galatians became one new person by being united with Christ Himself."[26]

Paul's conclusion? This life-altering relationship with Jesus transforms both our personal standing before God as well as our corporate positioning with one another.[27] The atoning death of Jesus overcame the tragic results of sin that separated human hearts from God and divided people from one another. Among his closing statements, Paul makes a ground-breaking declaration to his Galatian brothers and sisters. He announces, *"There is no longer Jew or Greek, there is no longer slave or free, there is no longer male or female; for all of you are one in Christ Jesus!"*[28] Not only has Jesus radically transformed our souls, He's also established a radically transformed society! One commentator aptly states, "Religious, social, and sexual pairs of opposites are not replaced by equality, but rather by a newly created unity in Jesus Christ."[29]

RADICAL UNITY

Let's take a closer look at Paul's powerful pronouncement. His statement begins with the phrase, "there is no longer." There's no uncertainty in this phrase. He's boldly declaring with finality that things have drastically changed. This is "an announcement of fact rather than a mere possibility."[30] As a wise spiritual father, Paul is exhorting his sons and daughters to adjust their relationships to a new kingdom order. Where Jesus is honored and His commands are followed, "there is unity and equality in diversity."[31]

Throughout Paul's letter to the Galatians, his focus is primarily on issues between Jews and Gentiles. Here in this statement, however, Paul broadens his comments to address divisions between slaves and freemen and men and women. At the time of the writing of this letter, Greco-Roman culture viewed "a wife as property of her husband, and her status ranked with slaves and children."[32] Josephus, a contemporary historian of that time period, described the cultural climate this way: "In every respect, woman is inferior to man."[33] Yet the Greeks and Romans weren't alone in their opposition to gender equality. The Jewish culture had its own expressions of ethnic, social, and gender biases. In Judaism, Gentiles and women had limited access to certain parts of the Temple areas.[34] In fact most of the Temple courts were forbidden to them. In addition, Jewish men greeted each day with this prayer, reinforcing the division that began in the Garden:

"Praise be to you, Adonai our God, King of the universe, because You have not made me a Gentile. Praise be to You, Adonai our God, King of the universe, because You have not made me a slave. Praise be to You, Adonai our God, King of

the universe, because You have not made me a woman."[35]

It's highly likely that Paul was regularly exposed to this prayer, even praying it himself in his former days as a Pharisee.[36] If you compare this prayer with Paul's declaration in Galatians 3:28, there's a significant correlation. In his statement to the Galatians, Paul uses the same chronological order as the morning prayer to declare, "In Christ all distinctions of superiority fade! Ethnic descent, social status, or gender have nothing to do with our present privilege!"[37] Paul is taking the traditional prayer and reversing its curses, breaking the chains of division. By the power of Jesus' death and resurrection, spirits of superiority and separation have been defeated. One summary of this threefold decree states, "It is not the force of man but the love of God which alone can unite a disunited world."[38]

Paul addresses these three divisions, once a vital part of his religious experience, and now "affirms that in Christ they are irrelevant."[39] He's purposeful in making this declaration, strongly reflected in his word choice. The phrase translated as, "there is no distinction," uses a specific noun form describing "equal honor extended to both parties."[40] In Jesus' Kingdom, women and men mutually honor one another. This oneness of men and women in Christ is a bond directly contrasting the relational turmoil Adam and Eve's sin created.[41] Jesus has fully demonstrated His power to "conquer all things and establish a new order."[42] Every social division common in any culture can now be radically transformed in Him.

It's important to note that this letter was written in a culture where marriage was predominantly based on contract, not mutual love and respect. In this society a wife's role was similar to that of a servant. She was often viewed as having two primary functions: to birth a male child, thus providing a lawful heir, and to manage the affairs of the household.[43] Therefore Galatians 3:28 is a shock to this culture, and any culture that makes value-based distinctions between people based on ethnicity, status, or gender.

Not all students of the scriptures, however, interpret this passage as a liberating decree for all people. One author writes, "Galatians 3:28 has to do with one's status before God, yet has nothing to do with functions in the church."[44] Those holding to this view see Jesus' transforming work as providing personal salvation, while minimizing His impact on our corporate relationships. For those who limit the effects of Galatians 3:28, "being one in Christ does not abolish different functions for male and female."[45] While acknowledging that every person can be equally justified before God through faith in Christ, those sharing this opinion feel that "male hierarchy in the home or in the church" should remain intact.[46]

Several questions arise in my heart when I hear this perspective. Is the freedom Jesus purchased for us a limited liberation? Can we stand mutually loved by God, yet remain dishonoring in our relationships with one another? "If a Gentile may exercise spiritual leadership in the church as freely as a Jew, or a slave as freely as a citizen, why not a woman as freely as a man?"[47]

The overwhelming message of the New Testament is that Jesus' atonement created a new order where men and women truly function as "members of one another."[48] Discrimination between women and men was removed when circumcision was discontinued as a sign of covenant. In its place, water baptism became the new sign of covenant, open to both genders indiscriminately.[49] Men and women receive the same justifying grace and, as demonstrated throughout the New Testament, share as "ministry partners in preaching the Gospel."[50]

In this amazing atmosphere, we fully become all we were created to be. Ancient divisions of superiority and inferiority are obliterated. Jesus established a gift-based—no longer gender-biased—culture in His Kingdom. In this climate, every member can freely fulfill their unique calling in Him. Much like facets of a diamond, the multidimensional members of Christ's Body will "reflect the beauty of the Christ-life, each from his or her own angle."[51] As the first man and woman were made in the likeness of God, so now, in the new creation, we reflect His glory as His corporate expression.

This termination of division between men and women was more than Paul's wishful fantasy. The New Testament accounts of Paul's ministry demonstrate his groundbreaking strides to transition Galatians 3:28 from a declaration to a demonstration. In Romans 16 he openly honors women as fellow teammates in ministry. His letter to the Corinthian churches encourages women to pray, to teach, and to prophesy side by side with their brothers.[52] Paul acknowledges that his own spiritual foundations were received from Priscilla, a powerful teacher.[53] Apollos, another apostle contemporary to Paul, also received significant training from this mighty woman of God.[54] Paul encouraged his spiritual son, Timothy, to recall the foundational instruction he had received from significant women in his life, namely his mother Eunice and his grandmother Lois.[55] In Paul's worldview, "both genders should equally participate in Christ by the Spirit."[56]

Galatians 3:26-29 is one of the most hope-filled texts in the Bible. The death and resurrection of Jesus made a way for all people, regardless of ethnicity, status, or gender, to fully experience mutual validation and purpose in His corporate body, the Church. For this to occur, true honor must be restored as a lifestyle among His people. Genuine respect cannot be coerced or legally enforced. It must flow from deep conviction and authentic love.

The passion behind Paul's Galatians 3:28 declaration should become ours, as well. We must insist that to be "one new person in Christ" means "all [of us] are mutually interdependent for life" in His body.[57] Born out of this conviction, author Fawn Parish states, "None of us come into our full destiny by ourselves. Honor promotes others.... Honor does not seek to restrain and exclude, but to enlarge and expand possibilities."[58] The body of Christ, according to Paul, prevails in a culture of honor in which every member can fully participate. In essence, women and men partner in ministry as they synergize their gifts and callings. The conviction of gender interdependence permeates Paul's writings, and must be kept in mind when interpreting several seemingly divisive statements in his other letters.

Let's take a look at one of them now.

CHAPTER 8

1 TIMOTHY 2:11-15 IN CONTEXT

"...handling accurately the word of truth."
2 Timothy 2:15 (NASB)

Any verse in the Bible can be removed from its context and made to support a variety of opinions. Isolated proof texts and biased interpretations can be used to support either side of the issue of women in ministry. In order for our discussion to move beyond endless debates, we must first establish a theology of ministry found in the heart of God who "gives gifts for ministry and is no respecter of persons."[1]

Currently there appears to be an absence of any middle ground concerning women in church leadership due to "a few highly debated biblical passages, first and foremost being 1 Timothy 2:11-15."[2] As we focus on this specific passage of scripture, it's important to keep in mind God's overarching design for men and women. Opponents of women in ministry often isolate this passage "with minimal acknowledgement of the roles of women in Scripture as a whole."[3] Context is crucial in any pursuit of truth. With this in mind, let's consider all we have discussed so far.

COLLABORATION IN CONTEXT

Starting with their creation, God clearly called the woman and the man to rule the earth together. In shared partnership, He fashioned them to be His image-bearers in the world. As Denise Jordan notes, "Both the man and the woman were appointed to have dominion in a synergy of the authority of love over the created order."[4] By creating man and woman in His image, God established a powerful force of unity between them. They shared dominion over the earth, with neither one being created or called to be superior to the other. Some have deduced a hierarchy in the creation account, however. Citing the fact that man was created first in the "order of creation," they conclude that "men bear God's image directly and women only indirectly; hence the priority of male over female."[5] However the words God spoke in creation don't reflect male superiority and female subjective servitude. God called the woman "a helper suitable for him."[6] This phrase literally means, "corresponding to him in a parallel partnership, not a subservient second-class role."[7] In their created state, there was no hierarchy or male authority over the female. They shared a glorious oneness, reflecting the very image of God.

Sadly, their sinful fall from grace severed their relationship with God and shattered their honoring comradery with one another. Future generations would suffer the bitter effects of their iniquitous rebellion. On the surface, the Old Testament appears to chronicle a strong, male-dominated order in Israelite society. The ideal wife watched over the affairs of the household,[8] while her husband joined his male peers at the gates, overseeing the political life in what appeared to be a male exclusive domain.[9]

However, closer inspection of the Old Testament discloses an apparent patriarchal system that was not so hierarchical that it excluded women from serving in leadership roles. A significant number of biblical stories record the exploits of spirited women contributing to the leadership of Israel. Yet these narratives "do not constitute the total number of women acting in such authoritative roles. Rather, the Old Testament gives every indication that unnamed women and men served in authoritative capacities throughout Israel's history."[10] In fact Old Testament records "give the clear impression that Israel acknowledged the authority of God-ordained women in leadership to the same extent of their male counterparts."[11] Closer examination of Old Testament scriptures "offers no evidence that the Israelites ever rejected a woman's leadership simply on the basis of gender."[12]

Though some levels of freedom and restoration were experienced by Old Testament believers, all of creation longed for a better covenant to be enacted. Ultimately, sin's grievous destruction was gloriously restored through Jesus' atoning sacrifice. His new covenant established a magnificent transformation. In His

Kingdom, there's now a fresh paradigm. In Jesus, hierarchical tiers give way to gender-inclusive peers. A once patriarchal system has now become a mutually honoring culture, releasing both men and women to serve and lead together in the church Jesus is building. Paul's socially explosive declaration in Galatians 3:28 brought radical freedom to every member of the church. Every part of Christ's body can now fully participate in their God-appointed roles.

New Testament support for the mutual gifting, calling, and operation of men and women together in ministry is quite visible.[13] Female ministry roles increased rapidly and steadily in the early church, with women serving as apostles,[14] prophets,[15] evangelists,[16] and pastoral overseers.[17] There wasn't a feminist equality movement. Nor did a resentful battle of the sexes erupt to prove worth or attain dominance. Rather, the daughters and sons of God united to fulfill Jesus' great commission, transforming nations with His Gospel. This wasn't a fight for equality, since all people are not equally gifted. It was a joint passion to see everyone utilizing their unique giftings to serve in their corporate calling. Neither men nor women appeared to claim exclusivity regarding giftedness. They seemed to understand that the gifts of the Holy Spirit are dispersed, not consolidated, among both women and men. There appears to be no scriptural precedent for the thought that the Holy Spirit makes gender a requirement for certain kinds of giftings. Rather, the

Bible "clearly indicates that the Holy Spirit has no gender-exclusive gifts."[18]

CHALLENGES IN CHURCH HISTORY

Though New Testament believers seemed to experience renewed comradery, the controversy over women serving with men in ministry leadership was not fully resolved with the early church. Theologians and ecclesiastical leaders throughout church history have had equally divergent opinions in this matter. Early church fathers such as Tertullian and Thomas Aquinas concluded that "women should not speak in the context of public worship services…or sing or pray audibly among men."[19] Concerning the oneness of men and women declared in Galatians 3:28, Saint Augustine, the Bishop of Hippo, stated, "This oneness regards our spiritual unity alone. This status has no correlation to united function in the church."[20] John Wesley, on the other hand, always allowed women to participate fully in his "class meetings. But he gave women permission to 'exhort' rather than 'preach.' He also advised them to call their gatherings 'prayer meetings,' lest anyone think they were forming a congregation with a female preacher."[21] Revivalist Charles Finney was similarly guarded in his endorsement of women in ministry. "Although Finney was open to the public ministry of women, he was by no means a vocal advocate of women's ordination."[22] Yet his reliance on the support of women for his revival meetings led him to conclude, "The church that silences women is shorn of half its power."[23]

Throughout the generations, the battle over women leaders in the church "has often found its epicenter in the interpretation of 1 Timothy 2:11-15. A hierarchical interpretation of this passage" has become the cornerstone for the prohibition of women in church leadership.[24] Because the understanding of this passage greatly impacts our theology of ministry, affecting both men and women, it's crucial for us to analyze these verses in context.

1 TIMOTHY 2:11-15

"A woman should learn in quietness and full submission. I do not permit a woman to teach or to assume authority over a man; she must be quiet. For Adam was formed first, then Eve. And Adam was not the one deceived; it was the woman who was deceived and became a sinner. But women will be saved through childbearing—if they continue in faith, love and holiness with propriety." 1 Timothy 2:11-15 (NIV)

Paul wrote this letter to young pastor Timothy, addressing important issues he was facing in his church at Ephesus. At the core of the document is Paul's strong caution for Timothy to "remain in Ephesus" so that he can "command certain people not to teach false doctrines any longer."[25] This issue is the focal point of the epistle, with over half of its content addressing the evils of false teaching. Paul's posture throughout the letter is corrective. His words are strong. The tone is stern, giving the sense that Timothy is encountering critical problems that require immediate attention. This factor prompts the question: "Is Paul correcting a specific issue in the Ephesian church? Or is he setting a precedent for all churches throughout all generations?"

It's helpful to consider the culture of the city in which Timothy and the church were planted. Ephesus in the first-century was a metropolis where women were "highly influenced by the cult of Artemis, in which the female was exalted and considered superior to the male."[26] The teaching of this sect propagated erroneous myths and ancestor worship—deceptive philosophies which Paul referred to as "godless chatter."[27] He warned Timothy of the subtle ways these false doctrines were successfully influencing the women of Ephesus.[28] This female cult taught that "Artemis, a female deity, appeared first and then her male partner was created second; used as proof of female superiority. This factor provides context to Paul's statement regarding God's order in creation in which Adam was formed first, then Eve."[29] In light of this, Paul appears to be correcting false teaching rather than promoting male superiority based on the order of creation.

In addition, women were taught to look to Artemis for protection during their childbirth. Therefore Paul's statement that "women will be kept safe through childbirth"[30] discourages women from trusting in a false god, while encouraging them to put their faith in Jesus.[31]

He's not saying that childbirth will ensure a woman's salvation, nor is he establishing women with children as superior to those who are childless. Ultimately, he's correcting their faith in a counterfeit deity.

Throughout this letter, Paul is also addressing lots of issues in the life of the Ephesian church, including immorality among leaders, family problems, and doctrinal heresies. Two church leaders had to be removed from office,[32] other elders had to be openly corrected,[33] malicious talk and constant friction had to be addressed,[34] and people who had "wandered from the faith" had to be restored.[35]

Paul is also writing in an effort to resolve the problem of disorderly conduct in public worship gatherings. Paul's appeal for peaceful behavior among women[36] seems to suggest women were disrupting their church assemblies. However, some of the men were equally causing tension in corporate settings by praying in an angry, contentious way.[37] In this context, Paul's words seem less like a desire to remove women from verbally contributing in church gatherings and more like an appeal to restore order to chaotic assemblies. As Mary Evans cites, "None of Paul's other letters that speak to the conduct of women in worship forms a basis for prohibiting women from serving in any aspect of church ministry."[38] One researcher observes, "In a church where women were illiterate, still impacted by the loud and lewd worship practices from their former involvement in matriarchal goddess cults, such a strong instruction makes sense. But in the majority of other churches, women had positions of prominence."[39] Once again, the question we must ask is, "Did Paul's words address a specific problem in a specific church at a specific time? Or is he laying down a mandate for all churches at all times?"

The most difficult clause to unpack is, "I do not permit a woman to teach or to have [exercise] authority over a man."[40] Paul's phrase "I do not permit" has caused some to interpret his strong words as a timeless mandate for all churches. Was Paul writing in a future universal sense or was he assisting a young pastor with a present problem? Closer examination of Paul's word choice can help us gain some clarity. The word translated "permit" is the Greek word *epitrepo*. It's a precise term, referring to "entrusting someone with a highly influential, mutually shared responsibility."[41] When this word is used in the Septuagint, the Greek translation of the Old Testament, it refers to a very specific, extremely trusted position having widespread impact.[42] Could it be that Paul is telling Timothy to guard places of strategic, doctrinal influence from the infiltration of women who were false teachers?

Another factor to consider is the verb tense of the word "permit." He uses the present tense, rather than the future tense, which may indicate that his decision has to do with resolving a current problem rather than "laying down a widespread prohibition against all leadership activities for all women."[43] In light of the specific nature of the word and the present tense of the verb, it appears that Paul's instructions "most likely had a specific and limited" application to circumstances at that time.[44] To take the correction needed in one incident and apply it to all people everywhere seems highly unfair. It could be compared to a father confining a wayward son to his room, and then indiscriminately placing every child under house arrest. As Randolph Richards cautions, "In the ancient world of the Bible, some rulings did not necessarily apply to 100 percent of the people. Specific tenets could concern specific situations. To the non-Western mind, a law is a guideline. Therefore, in our interpretations we should always leave room for exceptions."[45]

A greater consideration is the content and context of *all* of Paul's writings. Throughout the Pauline epistles, the issue of women teaching never seemed to be a concern for Paul. He acknowledged the instruction Timothy received from both his mother and grandmother.[46] Paul encouraged both men and women to counsel one another.[47] He commended both women and men for their ministry leadership contributions in Romans 16. He also encouraged both men and women to participate in the ministry of instruction,[48] as well as prophecy.[49] Therefore, we must consider whether Paul is prohibiting women from a specific kind of teaching, or forbidding them from all teaching of any kind. Strong opinions exist on both sides of this issue. Let's take a moment to consider both.

Bible scholar John Piper states, "We do not understand Paul to mean an absolute prohibition of all teaching by women. They can train younger women or male children within their families. As Priscilla taught at her husband Aquila's side, a woman may teach adults only when she is subordinate to her husband's ministry."[50] Piper continues, "While women may share prophetic words, the testing of these words and the regular teaching ministry in the church is the responsibility of male elder-teachers, a role assigned uniquely to men."[51]

The term that has caused this passage to be used to forbid women from taking leadership roles is *authentein*, a Greek word translated by some as, "exercising authority over a man."[52] The word *authentein* occurs only once—here—in the entire New Testament. It's sharply different from the common word for "authority," *exousia*, translated as "those who give care, cover in prayer, lead by example, and motivate by encouragement."[53] Some linguistic scholars translate *authentein* as a vile term describing "the perpetrator of a crime or an act of violence."[54] However, more recent and consistent translations see the word as a description of "ruling or dominating, usurping power or rights from another, and claiming ownership."[55] Richard Kroeger cites, "Unquestionably, 'to dominate' is a valid meaning of authentein."[56] Some scholars who have strong convictions opposing women in leadership have conceded, "We must acknowledge that *authentein* can be translated as 'to rule, to reign sovereignly, and to control or dominate.'"[57]

A number of Bible scholars I've admired for years are adamant about this passage serving as the cornerstone of male-only leadership in the church. James I.

Packer concludes, "Though we are unsure of how Paul would apply this text in our culture, we should give the apostle the benefit of the doubt and retain his restriction on women exercising authority over men in the church."[58] C.S. Lewis states, "Because an ordained minister stands in the place of God, representing God to the congregation, a woman cannot properly fulfill the pastoral office."[59] Others agree, while giving some leniency toward women teaching in the church, stating, "Paul is forbidding women to teach from the authority position of a pastor or elder. He is not hindering women from teaching. They simply should not serve in an office of authority."[60] John Piper summarizes, "1 Timothy 2:11-15 gives abiding sanction to an eldership of spiritual men. The headship of the husband at home leads naturally to the primary leadership of spiritual men in the church. Therefore, it is unbiblical and detrimental for women to assume this role."[61]

On the other hand, equally sincere scholars have very different views in this centuries-old controversy. The 1800's Holiness Movement leader, Phoebe Palmer, offers this wise advice: "Scripture is meant to be interpreted by Scripture. Serious errors in faith and practice result when isolated passages are used to sustain a pet theory."[62] Others agree, "We should not allow our traditions and uncertain interpretations of a single passage to deny the calling of women who otherwise prove themselves fit for ministry."[63] Still others simply state, "It is a very weak hermeneutic to use this passage to deprive women of leadership opportunities."[64]

Dr. Craig Keener makes this wise proposal "It would be surprising if an issue that would exclude at least half of the body of Christ from a ministry of teaching would be addressed in only one text, unless that text addressed only a specific historical situation rather than setting forth a universal prohibition."[65] Keener continues, "The admonition to stop talking and pay attention to what was being said need not mean that the person was forever to remain quiet. Paul, who wants women to 'learn quietly,' does not want them to teach disruptively."[66] He concludes, "Paul wants women to learn so that they could teach. If he prohibits women from teaching because they are unlearned, his demand that they learn constitutes a long-range solution."[67]

This interpretation is consistent with Paul's later instructions in 2 Timothy 2:2. There he encourages Timothy to entrust his teachings to reliable persons, *both* men *and* women, "who will also be qualified to teach others."[68] While some translations of 2 Timothy 2:2 read "faithful men,"[69] others say "reliable people."[70] The latter translation seems most accurate. Paul could have chosen to use the word *andros* in this statement, a term meaning "men only." However, Paul selected the word *anthropos*, which means *both* men *and* women. Paul would be highly inconsistent if, on one hand, he banned all women from teaching while, on the other hand, encouraging Timothy to expand his teaching ministry through qualified men *and* women.

Loren Cunningham summarizes his interpretation of 1 Timothy 2:11-15 with these sensible words, "Since there is a virtually unbroken tradition, from the oldest versions and running down to the twenty-first century, regarding the translation of *authentein* as 'to dominate to get one's way,' Paul's address to Timothy seems to be a corrective instruction toward a specific problem."[71] Paul's other letters, as well as his own practice of teaching side by side with anointed women, show that he fully acknowledged and supported his sisters in ministry. Therefore, Paul isn't pronouncing an eternal ban on women teaching and serving with men in leadership in the church. Instead, he's addressing an unhealthy situation in the Ephesian congregation, namely specific women who were seeking to dominate and deceive others. As Kris Vallotton highlights, "Throughout 1 Timothy, Paul calls both genders to align their attitudes to the will of God, without singling out women as the only ones requiring an attitude adjustment."[72]

CONCLUSION

From creation, it's been the design and desire of God for women and men to relate, rule, and reflect His glory *together*, in mutually honoring relationships. In spite of the first couple's rebellion against His purposes, He has never changed His heart toward us, nor His plans for us. One author clearly describes the power of our togetherness this way: "Women and men together reflect the image of God. Therefore, He intends for women and men to serve together in all aspects of church life."[73] Christine Caine articulates, "The history of our world—in all periods of time, on all continents, and in all cultural traditions—is rampant with damage, oppression, diminishment, and hostility aimed at women. Of all places on earth, the Christian church should be the most significant place of healing and hope."[74]

There are those who would argue that women who lead and teach in the church are not properly submitted, citing Paul's words in 1 Timothy 2:11 requiring women to be "in full submission."[75] It's insightful to note the "full submission" called for in this verse is usually taken to mean women submitting to men, but most likely it's a call for submission to God.[76] Thus the woman called by God to ministry must respond to God, refusing to relinquish her calling to the people who forbid her. Mary, the mother of Jesus, brought history-making significance "through her obedience, not to a man, not to a culture…but to the creative work of God" in her life.[77] All women are not to be submitted to all men. Women as a gender are not inferior to or under the rule of men. "A married woman should be submissive to her own husband by not usurping his authority, but this does not apply to her relationship with other men."[78] Healthy marriages are marked by mutual submission to one another, as husbands and wives ultimately submit to Jesus as Lord of their home.[79] It is ultimately our submission to God that will result in the fulfillment of His purposes on earth through every member of His family.

It's vital for every member, both women and men, to experience equal opportunities to fulfill their God-given callings. God's word clearly presents ministry roles and responsibilities as gift-based, not gender-biased, infusions from the Holy Spirit—who freely gives unique empowerments without discrimination. As adopted sons and daughters, everyone must fully access their spiritual inheritance, free from the constraints of limiting translations of God's liberating word. As Loren Cunningham challenges, "We must champion the right of women and men to choose the call of God in their lives and give more and more people the opportunity to serve the Body with all their gifts."[80]

CHAPTER 9

WHAT ABOUT THOSE OTHER VERSES?

"It is time for us to rethink some of our oldest beliefs and traditions. It is time for us to repent for whatever ways we have hindered God's work and misread His Word. It is time for us to release women to be all that God has called them to be."

–Loren Cunningham

Although 1 Timothy 2:11-15 is by far the most quoted and controversial scripture in the debate over women in ministry leadership, there are a few other New Testament verses that can be problematic. Let's consider some of them.

"AN OVERSEER MUST BE...THE HUSBAND OF ONE WIFE." 1 TIMOTHY 3:2 (ESV)

The debate over the meaning of this verse may not simply be over its content. It may also be its placement, one chapter after 1 Timothy 2:11-15. For those interpreting the previous passage as a prohibition, 1 Timothy 3:2 follows as a reinforcement. For them, this explanation seems obviously pointed: "Only men can lead. And only married men can lead." Yet this view raises several valid questions. Is Paul forbidding additional groups from teaching and leadership roles? Is he also prohibiting single men from serving as overseers? According to most Bible scholars, Paul and Timothy were both unmarried. So it would be highly unlikely—and inconsistent—for Paul to make marriage a prerequisite for leadership.

Another pertinent question: Does Paul's reference to an overseer being "the husband of one wife" further solidify a ban on women in leadership? While the phrase is male-exclusive, the other character traits listed in this passage are qualities of godly leaders, whether they're male or female.

This raises the question: If Paul was listing standards for both genders in leadership, why does the phrase "the wife of one husband" not appear? Once again, the historical context of Paul's letters is crucial in the interpretation process. Sexual immorality and marital infidelity were commonplace in the Graeco-Roman culture. Prostitution was "an integral part of society in Corinth, Ephesus, Athens, and Rome."[1] Jewish moral principles of sexual purity within the covenant of marriage were despised and dismissed within the Roman world. For this reason, many of Paul's letters include strong warnings to resist moral compromise.

Male polygamy was also legal in this culture. However, despite blatant indifference to the sanctity of marriage, there's no historical record of women having multiple husbands. For this reason, "Paul insisted that a male bishop or deacon have only one wife."[2] Female polygamy simply was not an issue in that era. Therefore, the "husband of one wife" phrase does not say, "Only men can be overseers." It simply states that men who are overseers must be in covenant with only one wife.

Another important consideration in the interpretation of 1 Timothy 3 is the grammar Paul used. He begins this chapter with the phrase, "If anyone aspires to be an overseer...."[3] The noun "anyone" is not a masculine term. It literally indicates *anyone*, both male or female. Most translations use the term "he" throughout the passage, most likely to be consistent with the "husband of one wife" phrase. However, using "he or she" and "his or her" throughout this passage would hold more accurately to Paul's grammatical choice.[4] The question then arises, "What about the phrase 'if a *man* knows how to rule his own house'?[5] Isn't that a male-exclusive statement?" Interestingly, the word translated as "man" is the Greek word tis, referred to as "an indefinite pronoun," indicating "some or any person," either male or female, individual or several.[6] Thus the address could be seen as stressing the importance of overseers, either mothers or fathers, effectively leading their families and the church. Reading 1 Timothy 3 in its entirety supports the very clear impression that Paul is addressing character qualities vital to both men and women serving as leaders. However, there's another verse in this passage that can bring some clarity.

"LIKEWISE, THEIR WIVES MUST BE REVERENT." 1 TIMOTHY 3:11 (KJV)

This verse, addressed to servant leaders (i.e., deacons), can appear to say that only men can be deacons, and their wives must be respectable. Yet several factors should be considered as we ponder the meaning of this verse. The word *likewise* is similar to "a literary equal sign; it means 'in the same way.'"[7] Paul is explaining, in effect, "What I am saying to the men I am also saying to the women. In your leadership roles in the church, all of you must be godly examples." Without exception, "Paul treated men and women the same, as coworkers in the Gospel."[8]

Another factor is the word often translated as "wives." Paul uses the Greek word *gune*, meaning "a woman of any age, whether a virgin, married, or widowed."[9] Some versions have captured this distinction, using the word "women" instead of "wives."[10] Other versions have added the word "their" to the translation, a word that does not appear in the original language. By doing this, the meaning can be skewed to say that only married women could serve *if* their husbands were leaders. However, by using the general term *gune*, Paul is opening the door for *all women* to serve with men in leadership.

Just as Paul brought correction to some women who were disruptive,[11] he's now bringing instruction to women who are distinctive. Paul restores the damage done by female false teachers "by stating the qualities for godly women to be released into public ministry."[12] The structure of this letter suggests that Paul's intention is to overcome evil with good, deception with truth, and abuse with godly leadership by releasing both men and women as Christlike colleagues in ministry.

Another important dynamic in this passage are the words commonly translated as "overseer or bishop" and "deacon." *Episcopas* is a generic word for leaders, meaning "to watch over" or "overseers who serve."[13] *Diakonos*, at times translated as "deacon," was commonly used to "emphasize the servant character of New Testament leadership."[14] Long before turning the words "bishop" and "deacon" into authoritative offices, these were everyday words used by Paul to describe the compassionate care and courageous encouragement servant leaders brought to the church. They weren't words of privilege and power. Rather they described the true heart of a leader to assist and empower others.

Much of the discussion surrounding women in ministry often has little to do with the issue of ministry, and more to do with the issue of authority. "Who's in charge?" can appear to be our greatest concern. How contrary to the fact that Jesus places leaders within His fellowship "to equip the saints for the work of ministry."[15] Leaders are called to "facilitate the ministry of the entire community."[16]

The ministry of "overseers," *episkopos*, is almost always related to administrating and coordinating congregational ministry—literally "to add to the mission."

The emphasis is on the mission of the church, not on titles or entitlement. True leaders have hearts to serve. They don't create or demand "seats of honor."[17] A passion to *complete* our corporate mission leaves no room for us to compete for power. Men and women leaders must freely use whatever gifts the Holy Spirit gives them to equip others. These gifts have been wisely and widely distributed throughout the church by the Holy Spirit; and many women carry administrative gifts which are desperately needed to coordinate churches and ministries. As Paul said, it's a "good thing" for women and men with leadership gifts to "aspire" to use those gifts "for the common good."[18] From my vantage point, there's no evidence in 1 Timothy 3 to imply "that the Spirit applies gender considerations in appointing any of the gifts, including the gift of leadership."[19]

With this in mind, let's consider one more passage that can appear to immobilize women.

> *"Women should remain silent in the churches. They are not allowed to speak, but must be in submission, as the law says. If they want to inquire about something, they should ask their own husbands at home; for it is disgraceful for a woman to speak in the church."* 1 Corinthians 14:34-36 (NIV)

Once again, the question we must ask is, "Does Paul intend to endlessly silence all women in the church? Or is he bringing correction to a specific situation, in a specific church, at a specific time?" We must keep in mind that this is a letter written to the Corinthian church, providing needed instructions for their unique circumstances. We benefit today from the timeless truths contained in this ancient, Spirit-inspired epistle. However, forming assumptions without considering context has caused significant errors throughout church history.

One of the major themes in this letter concerns division and confusion, a demonic strategy threatening to derail this church. An area of contention appears to be the strife between men and women. Paul boldly challenges them to embrace the God-given interdependence of the genders. Addressing their independent spirit, he said, "In the Lord, however, woman is not independent of man, nor is man independent of woman."[20]

He encouraged them to pursue loving relationships with one another, while eagerly desiring the Holy Spirit's ministry among them.[21] Frequently, Paul used corporate language as he challenged them to break down walls of division between them. He said, "I would like *every one of you* to speak in tongues."[22] He encouraged, "You can *all* prophesy."[23] He gave specific instructions for ways both men and women should participate openly and verbally in their corporate gatherings.[24] "When Paul makes statements like 'you all' or 'every one of you,' he is speaking to the entire church," not excluding women from the invitation.[25] With this in mind, it raises the valid question, "Why would Paul exhort men and women to minister together publicly, and then relegate the women to total silence in their meetings?"

This letter was written to correct moral compromise and theological error in the Corinthian church. It was also scribed to confront division and confusion in their ranks. Disorder crept into their fellowship, causing great disarray in their worship services and Lord's Supper celebrations.[26] Paul's fatherly wisdom clearly addressed the confusion. His main thought could be summarized, "Since God is a God of order, all should participate in Christian worship in an orderly and edifying way."[27]

Paul addressed three groups of people who were causing disorder in the church: those who were continually speaking in tongues,[28] others who were interrupting with their prophesying,[29] and women who were disrupting the services with their outbursts.[30] For all three of these groups, Paul gave the same instruction. Those perpetually speaking in tongues were told they "should keep quiet."[31] The ones prophetically interfering with others were informed they "should stop."[32] And the unruly women were directed to "remain silent."[33] Paul repeated the same word to each group: simply "be silent."

In this passage, "be silent" involved taking turns,[34] listening to one another,[35] and being self-controlled, so that "everyone could be instructed and encouraged."[36] Paul was not intending to eliminate tongues, terminate prophecy, or prohibit women from ever participating in corporate gatherings. His goal was not to limit ministry, but to enhance it. His call to silence these instances of disorder should not be interpreted as an eternal moratorium on women in ministry.

The fact that the women in question were speaking up out of a sincere desire to learn reveals their spiritual hunger. Despite their naivete, Paul recommends a fatherly solution: "Husbands, teach them."[37] He was not shutting them down. Instead, he was offering them a healthy remedy—to receive instruction so they could participate side by side with their husbands.

This invitation to be trained was radical in the Graeco-Roman world. "Women had little or no educational opportunities among the Greeks and Romans. The Jews also excluded women from study, including formal religious training."[38] It's sad to see this transforming word, giving women the redemptive opportunity to be instructed, interpreted as an indication that women are unfit for ministry. Paul was anything but dismissive toward these women. He fully expected their husbands to take responsibility and spend time bringing their wives up to speed. If their wives longed to learn, the husbands should patiently teach. Paul's ultimate desire was not to silence these women. He wanted them, with their husbands' help, to discover the joys of their unity in Christ and the delight of shared ministry.

For this reason, the final statement in this passage is troubling. The phrase, "It is disgraceful for a woman to speak in the church," seems abrupt. It also appears inconsistent with Paul's posture toward women throughout the letter. Earlier, he affirmed women as reflecting the glory of God to both men and angels.[39] He encouraged both men and women to prophesy in a respectful way. He inspired them to come to corporate meetings anticipating the possibility they may have a word of encouragement, a song, or a revelation to contribute to the gathering. All of this would involve verbal expression. Why then would Paul use such a harsh word as "disgraceful," a term meaning "shameful or filthy,"[40] to describe a woman's speech?

While this would be inconsistent with Paul's views of women, it clearly reflects the sentiment of the society of that time. Both the Romans[41] and the rabbis[42] frequently made such disparaging remarks about the voices of women. Therefore, it's very likely that Paul was quoting a common, cruel phrase. Since this letter was written in response to one he received from the Corinthian church leaders,[43] Paul may even have been repeating a statement contained in their letter. His reply, however, reflects his strong disapproval of this statement.

A small grammatical article begins the next sentence: "What!?!"[44] It could also be translated as "nonsense" or "ridiculous," obviously expressing his disagreement. The following rhetorical questions support this view: "Did the word of God originate with you? Are you the only people it has reached?"[45] Clearly, he's challenging them to reconsider their perspective. Though he is correcting disorderly women *and* men, Paul is unflinching in his passion to stop gender division in its tracks.

His conclusion of this chapter brings a wise resolve to the issues at hand. "Everything should be done in a fitting and orderly way,"[46] he writes. Disorderly men and women should be silent. Men and women should come to corporate worship services prepared to contribute. They should sing, prophesy, and encourage one another, using self-control as they minister. They should seek education and training, both men and women, so that they may minister more effectively. "For God is not a God of disorder but of peace."[47]

CHAPTER 10

A TALE OF TWO WOMEN

"Remember the days of old. Consider the years of many generations."
Deuteronomy 32:7 (ESV)

Researching the history of women in ministry in the American church can be quite heartbreaking. By comparison, there are far fewer records of the contributions made by females than the numerous accounts of male involvement. As one researcher says, when it comes to studying the spread of Christianity in the Western Hemisphere, "the women seem to have simply disappeared."[1] Some have seen this as confirmation of the lack of gifting and calling for women to lead. Others, however, have interpreted this trend as an indication of male discrimination and dominance.[2] For them, the minimal inclusion of females in historical records suggests that "women have been judged by the male standard of success, often assumed to be the only standard of success."[3]

Through the centuries, some historians have recorded the advances made by mighty women of God and their faithful male colleagues. Their stories include widely diverse moments, from powerful breakthroughs to painful setbacks. They chronicle accounts of vibrant faith and undaunted tenacity in the face of frequent misunderstanding and marginalization. As one historian describes, "During its 2,000-year journey, much of the church has accepted the view that women are subordinate to men based on the creation story in Genesis and the writings of Paul."[4] The thought of ever changing this viewpoint has been met with resistance throughout the church's history. To this day, many men appear to be oblivious to the experiences of many women in the church, especially women who are gifted to teach and to lead. As Danny Silk aptly says, "They either still think women belong in the 'submissive' role, or they think equality is already a reality. Either way, they see no need for real change."[5]

The issue of the appropriate roles for women in ministry has been debated in church circles for centuries. The terms used to identify the two primary positions are "egalitarian" and "complementarian." The egalitarian position promotes equal roles for men and women in ministry through mutual submission to one another. The complementarian view maintains that "men and women have corresponding roles that must function together, but only under male headship."[6] There is yet another opinion that women should be given no ministry responsibility other than the raising of their own children. These contrasting opinions are evident in the stories and experiences of Christian women throughout the ages.

I encountered many of these women in my survey of church history. Two of them especially caught my attention. Their tenacity and bravery are inspiring. Their zeal and grace are commendable.

Anne Hutchinson played a significant role in the early settlement of the Puritan era in American history during the 1600s. Her spiritual fervor and extensive theological training helped pave the way for future women ministers. Though Anglo-American, her example impacted women of all ethnicities for years to come. One such woman, Jarena Lee, was equally stirred to pursue her call to preach the gospel almost two centuries later. Both women, separated by many years and divergent cultures, played a vital role in the spiritual history of the church in America. Here are their stories.

During the early 1600s more than 20,000 Puritans migrated to what would become the United States of America. The culture of the Puritan community wasn't one of religious freedom, especially for women. Female members experienced "extreme oppression, similar to Sharia law within radical Islam."[7] As the century progressed, the oppression of women who aspired to ministry increased.[8] Women were excommunicated from the church by Puritan leaders for having Bible studies in their homes, for disbelieving that God spoke exclusively to the clergy, or for considering that "women could also hear from God."[9] Prominent women who were leading ministries were accused of witchcraft by a coalition of Puritan clergy and government officials.[10] Yet many, if not most, of those accused of being witches had no involvement in occult activity. In fact "any woman who claimed to have seen a vision or to have heard the voice of God was in danger of being executed as a sorceress."[11] During this tumultuous period of church history, Anne Hutchinson emerged as a shining example of the courage of early American ministry pioneers.

ANNE HUTCHINSON (1591-1643)

Anne was born in England in 1591, the daughter of Anglican minister Francis Marbury. Her father gained the reputation of being "an outspoken leader in his criticism of the established church and its appointment of unworthy pastors by the indifferent hierarchy."[12] Early in her life, Anne learned the importance of thinking independently and seeking discernment from the Lord. Because of her father's commitment to studying the Bible, Anne received a better theological education than most young women of her time.[13] Taught by her father, Anne gained a thorough understanding of the scriptures, "infused with seeds of independence and the courage to challenge clerical authority."[14]

In 1611, one year after her father's death, Anne married William Hutchinson, a successful merchant. Anne gave birth to fifteen children, causing a Puritan leader to observe, "To have survived so many pregnancies required considerable physical and mental strength."[15] Such tenacity typified Anne's life and ministry, equipping her to withstand fierce opposition without wavering in her convictions.

Anne deeply missed her late father's spiritual oversight. Their devotion to praying and pondering the scriptures had been a source of accelerated spiritual growth. Anne soon found a substitute for her father's mentorship, submitting herself to the spiritual instruction of the Reverend John Cotton, a Puritan pastor.[16] Under his guidance, Anne grew remarkably in "both knowledge and wisdom, especially in her ability to distinguish true preachers from false."[17] With Reverend Cotton's approval, Anne began to host Bible studies in her home. The meetings, known as "conventicles," attracted a wide array of spiritual seekers "to discuss sermons, debate dark places in scripture, and to pray."[18] Anne was not the only one hosting such meetings. Other church members, both men and women, were inspired by Anne to gather in groups in their own homes. As the conventicles grew, so did the disapproval of the clergy. "All of the home studies were frowned upon by the church hierarchy."[19] Their greatest grievance was the fact that "women played an active role in such assemblies, finding opportunity to speak out and exert the religious leadership denied them within the structure of the church."[20]

In 1633 John Cotton moved to Boston to pastor the first church of the new Boston Colony. The following year, prompted by Anne's sense that it was God's will for them to move, the Hutchinson family travelled to America to join Reverend Cotton and the fledgling

Boston Colony.[21] Anne's family easily accepted the rigors of relocation because they trusted her ability to hear the voice of God.[22]

Anne's husband, William, quickly experienced favor with the Boston authorities. His leadership skills opened the door for him to serve in various legislative positions. In a similar way, Anne received immediate access into the community, gaining respect especially among women "for her midwifery and childcare."[23] Her "outgoing personality and concern for the sick" deeply connected her to the community as she "devoted many hours serving those in need."[24] Yet her greatest respect came from her spiritual leadership as she "encouraged many of the women and their husbands to inquire more seriously after the Lord Jesus."[25] During her visits throughout the colony, many men and women were interested in Anne's revelations, "especially her emphasis on experiencing the transforming nature of conversion."[26] As Pastor Joseph Cotton observed Anne's success in ministry he noted, "The people's appetite for religious stimulation was generally unmet in the stoic religious structure" of Puritanism.[27] As a result, a growing number of people desired to participate in Anne's teaching sessions. Because the church leaders had not yet placed restrictions on the conventicle gatherings, Anne began to host "twice weekly meetings in her home."[28] They often studied the sermons of Joseph Cotton, but Anne also shared her own insights, as well as her personal criticisms of other ministers.[29]

Anne was known as a courageous woman, both revered and feared, because she was deemed "an intelligent and learned person, determined to remake the church."[30] She was known for her "remarkable vigor and charisma that might have changed the course of Massachusetts history had she been a man."[31] Anne inspired other Puritan women, "either by statement or by implicit example, to rebel against the roles they were expected to fulfill."[32] The prescribed roles of Puritan women limited them to "housekeeping and bearing and rearing children."[33] Women were "urged to avoid books and intellectual exercise" by Puritan leaders, because "such activity might overtax their weak minds."[34] These and other restrictions were based on their interpretation of "the instructions of Apostle Paul commanding each woman to hold her tongue in church, to be careful not to teach or usurp male authority, but to be in silence."[35] Puritan men used the scriptures to exclude women from all ministry, as John Cotton noted, "negating the idea that both men and women were brought to a direct experience of the Holy Spirit in equal measures."[36] In spite of such harsh discrimination, Anne Hutchinson was a spiritual pioneer, raising the bar for others to fully realize their God-given potential.[37] She was not an angry feminist seeking revenge on her male counterparts. Rather she rose as a symbol of freedom for both men and women to fulfill their callings. Together.

Though her outgoing personality and forthright speech often clashed with the reserved image expected of Puritan women, Anne's controversial teachings were the source of constant conflict with church leaders. They resisted Anne's emphasis on personal intimacy with God by teaching that "each person could be guided by his or her own conscience and inner morality."[38] They were equally enraged by her claim that "each person could communicate directly with God, without the need of outside supervision."[39] The "most troublesome idea" for the church hierarchy was Anne's conviction that "the person of the Holy Spirit dwells in every justified person," thus giving them "direct access to knowing the will of God."[40] At this point, the leaders deemed Anne a "heretic" whose teachings "threatened the view of the Bible as the sole source of truth."[41] Their ultimate concern appeared to be the way "Hutchinson's views threatened the authority of the colony's most important leaders, namely the clergy."[42]

Eventually the Boston colony was split into two parties, with one side embracing the views of Anne and the "Hutchinsonians," as they came to be called, and the other side pledging loyalty to the Boston church and its hierarchy.[43] One church leader described Anne as "a woman of ready wit and bold of spirit, who brought over with her two dangerous errors: First, that the person of the Holy Ghost dwells in every person. Secondly, that true sanctification is a work of the Holy Ghost and not merely the result of human effort alone."[44] In Anne's opinion, the church was "legalistic and slighted the work of the Holy Spirit" by placing "too high a value on human effort, which ultimately "encouraged false confidence and a haughty spirit."[45]

In her estimation, the clergy was guilty of "preaching a covenant of works."[46]

Underlying the resistance to Anne was the opinion that she had assumed a role of leadership contrary to scripture and in direct opposition to God's designed role for women. Hugh Peters, a church leader and bitter opponent of Anne, is quoted as saying, "You have stept out of your place. You have rather bine a Husband than a Wife and a Preacher than a Hearer, and a Magistrate than a Subject."[47] The church leaders accused Anne of two heresies: First, that she promoted "antinomianism," the belief that "since the saints are under the law of grace, the moral law was not binding on them anymore."[48] Second, that she and her followers were "familists," equating them with a 16th century religious sect known as "The Family of Love," who were falsely accused of "widespread promiscuity."[49] As time progressed it was determined that the followers of Anne Hutchinson were neither antinomian nor familists.[50] However, the damage was done and the lines were drawn.

The severe divide between the Puritan leaders and Anne Hutchinson heightened in 1635 as a fresh wave of British clergy came to Boston. Led by the Reverend John Wilson, John Cotton's senior overseer, the leadership solidified its opposition toward Anne and her followers. On the surface, it appeared to be a matter of doctrinal differences. But Puritan clergy "exaggerated the views of Anne's groups, accusing them of heresy in order to further quench her ministry."[51] With these blatant and detrimental remarks, the clash between them came to a heated conclusion.

In November of 1637, Anne went to trial before the General Court of Boston Colony, a trial that has since been called "one of the most dramatic moments of early American history."[52] According to court documents, the proceedings focused on "the threatening nature of her leadership influence in the colony among both men and women."[53] Anne was accused of being "the head of all this faction" and the "breeder and nourisher of all these distempers," and was charged with "dishonoring the authority of the ministers."[54]

As she was being challenged, Anne spoke openly of her spiritual history, her visions, and her cherished revelations from the Lord.[55] At the close of the trial Anne stated to the magistrate, "If you do condemn me for speaking what in my conscience I know to be the truth, I must commit myself to the Lord."[56] Her claim of having received "direct revelation from God" ended the trial and sealed her fate.[57] In March of 1638 Anne was found guilty of heresy by the Boston church and was formally excommunicated from the Boston Colony.[58] At that point, Reverend John Cotton severed his affiliation with Anne and her theology, viewed by some as "a weak concession to avoid excommunication."[59] Though wounded, Anne did not quit.

William and Anne Hutchinson, their family, and friends relocated to the Aquidneck Island on the Narragansett Bay, purchasing land from the Narragansett tribe. There they trained people to discern the voice of God and minister prophetically to one another.[60] For Anne, the shame of excommunication and the stress of relocation did not quench her continued devotion to ministry. Following William's death in 1642, Anne and six of her children moved to the Dutch colony of New Netherlands. One year later, all of the family, except the youngest daughter, were killed in a raid by a native tribe.[61]

Some saw Anne as a divisive heretic, while others saw her as a heroic defender of women's rights. For many, however, Anne was "a strong, intelligent, and witty woman; a worthy opponent of the best theological minds in her day."[62] Her valiant devotion to the call of Jesus on her life motivated her to finish her race and inspired future generations of godly women to pursue their spiritual calling.

JARENA LEE (1783-1855)

Two centuries after Anne Hutchinson finished her race, women like Jarena Lee still had to fight an uphill battle to fulfill what God had called them to do. Jarena Lee, and the men and women she inspired, became a powerful company of exhorters and preachers and spiritual climate-changers. Together they "spurred the formation of a web of interlocking social reform movements that changed the face of American culture."[63]

Minister Jarena Lee was the first woman licensed to preach by the African Methodist Episcopal (A.M.E.)

Church.[64] She was born to a poor, but free, black family on February 11, 1783 in Cape May County, New Jersey. At age seven, she was sent to work as a live-in servant for a white family. She moved to Philadelphia as a teenager, where she continued to work as a domestic servant. There she was "converted to Christianity and filled with the Holy Spirit after being inspired by the powerful preaching of Bishop Richard Alan, the founder of the A.M.E. Church."[65]

In 1807 Jarena heard the voice of God commissioning her to preach the Gospel, but "given the male-dominated nature of the church, she was reluctant to pursue the ministry."[66] When Lee confided in Bishop Alan her call to preach, he told her he could not grant her permission to preach due to the A.M.E.'s official ban against female ministers.[67] Dejected by her church's rejection, Jarena turned her heart toward homemaking, marrying Pastor Joseph Lee in 1811 and raising their two children in the following years.[68] Seven years later Lee's husband died, a turning point in Jarena's life as "her desire to proclaim the word of God grew even stronger."[69]

In 1819, during a worship service at Bethel A.M.E. Church, guest preacher Reverend Richard Williams began struggling with his sermon and abruptly stopped speaking. Lee sprang to her feet and began preaching, proceeding where the minister had ended his message.[70] In her own words, Jarena described this experience:

I sprang, as by altogether supernatural impulse, to my feet, when I was aided from above to give an exhortation on the very text which my brother Williams had taken...I told them I was like Jonah: for it had been nearly eight years since the Lord had called me to preach His gospel to the fallen sons and daughters of Adam's race, but that I had lingered like Jonah delayed to go at the bidding of the Lord, and warn those who were deeply guilty as were the people of Nineveh.[71]

The other pastors in the meeting responded as if the Lord Himself had spoken to their hearts. Bishop Alan was so impressed by Lee's exhortation that he "officially authorized her to preach the Gospel shortly thereafter."[72] Bishop Alan later wrote in his journal, "Jarena Lee was called to preach the gospel as much as any of the male preachers present."[73] From that time forward, Lee began to travel to various cities for preaching engagements and "was highly praised for her powerful sermons."[74] Yet like other women called to preach at that time, Jarena realized that God's call on her life "revealed a problem with women's limited roles in the church."[75]

As an African American woman, Jarena experienced obstacles to her ministry in both the racial arena, as well as the gender battlefront. Yet her enduring faith guarded her heart amid the onslaught of disapproval. She wrote in her journal, "On one occasion I met an older white man who told me, 'I do not believe the colored people have any souls.' However, after my sermon, he told me he had changed his mind."[76]

Jarena was equally fearless when facing misogynous accusations. Some of her opponents "spread the rumor that Jarena Lee was a man in woman's clothing."[77] Yet Jarena continually found the Lord to be her best defense, often quoting the promise: "When the Tempter raises a flood against you, God will set up a standard against him."[78] Though some misinterpreted her spiritual boldness as "prideful individualism," she was said to carry herself "serenely confident as a result of her relationship with the Holy Spirit."[79] She continually gave the Holy Spirit credit for giving her "an unanswerable legitimation from God"[80] that guarded her heart from demeaning undercurrents. Jarena used the terms "holy energy" and "holy boldness" to describe the tenacity God gave her amid "internal misgivings and the vigorous opposition of others."[81] She experienced what she described as "the Spirit-infused capacity to overcome timidity and the man-fearing spirit."[82]

Jarena Lee preached throughout New England, Canada, and Ohio, traveling by stagecoach, by boat, and on foot to minister in churches, schools, homes, camp meetings, and town halls.[83] Her influence impacted both the church culture as well as other social structures. Lee was one of the few African American women preaching prior to the abolition of slavery and the Civil War.[84] Joining the American Antislavery Society, Jarena synergized her gifts with others to abolish slavery.[85]

During her later years, Jarena traveled less and began to publish excerpts from her journals and other insights from her ministry years. Inspired to chronicle her life and ministry, Jarena saw her pen as a way "to make record of His holy influence available to a dying world."[86] Her story has been called "a testimony to God's providential care for an independent black woman in a racist and sexist society."[87] In giving advice to other female pioneers who would follow her, Lee said, "You will not let what a man may say or do, keep you from doing the will of the Lord or using the gifts you have for the good of others. How much easier to bear the reproach of men than to live at a distance from God."[88]

Beyond the conflict surrounding issues of race and gender, Jarena fought an even greater battle with faithless intellectualism. Much of her autobiography records "marvelous visions...and adventures as she followed the Holy Spirit's leading."[89] Such miraculous events opposed, as Lee described, "an atmosphere of worldly wisdom, self-sufficient reason, and opinionated faith" that permeated the church culture.[90] She frequently battled an intellectual skepticism among male church leaders who labeled "supposed miraculous phenomena" as excessive "female religious experiences" void of sound reason.[91]

Jarena completed her autobiography in 1836, and printed an expanded version in 1849.[92] Over 2,000 copies of her story were widely distributed, stirring both men and women to seek spiritual renewal and to desire social transformation.[93] The exact dates and circumstances of Minister Jarena Lee's death are unknown, but records of Mount Pisgah A.M.E. Church Cemetery where she is buried simply state that she died in 1855.[94]

CONCLUSION

It was holy inspiration, not merely human desperation, that motivated women like Anne Hutchinson and Jarena Lee to preach. It's been said that they "found God's encouragement more persuasive than society's discouragement."[95] These two women were not seeking to forward the cause of women as their primary goal. Their motivation was born out of deep conviction. Their focus was on the powerful role of the Holy Spirit and their longing for all to experience Him.

Though born centuries apart and worlds apart, these women shared much in common. First, they were exuberantly grateful for their new life in Christ. With genuine compassion and unquenchable faith, they sought to make Him known to all who would receive Him. Secondly, they responded wholeheartedly to the sobering call of God on their lives. Despite resistance from religious traditionalists, insecure misogynists, and blatant racists, they persevered by allowing the fear of God to replace the fear of man. Finally, they embraced their gender as a God-given component of their calling. They refused to adapt to the false notion that women were ancillary to the move of God.

Arguments against the ministries of women are seldom confined to gender issues. "Historically, they're attacks on the prophetic, Spirit-empowered view of ministry that the Pentecostal movement inherited from Phoebe Palmer and adopted as its own."[96] Palmer, an influential teacher in the Pentecostal Holiness movement of the nineteenth century, led wisely alongside her male colleagues. Phoebe insisted, "Because women as well as men received the fulness of the Holy Spirit, women as well as men are empowered to preach and prophesy together, with equal authority."[97] Attacks on women's right to lead and minister seem to coincide with cessationist desires to quench the activity of the Holy Spirit. Phoebe Palmer observes, "When the church loses its spiritual fervor, the ministries of women go into decline."[98] Palmer continues, "Those who decide that women should not be ministers usually have no value for the prophetic ministry, either."[99] Historically, during seasons of lifeless intellectualism in the institutional church, male-dominant leaderships have "devised theologies to justify both the absence of power and the secondary status of women."[100] This has profound application to our current opportunities. Living in days of tremendous spiritual potential for cultural transformation, we need to "receive fresh outpourings of the Holy Spirit as well as embrace the ministry of women He has anointed."[101]

CHAPTER 11

THEIR STORIES

"For his 'body' has been formed in his image and is closely joined together and constantly connected as one. And every member has been given divine gifts to contribute to the growth of all; and as these gifts operate effectively throughout the whole body, we are built up and made perfect in love."

Ephesians 4:16 (TPT)

Anne Hutchinson and Jarena Lee invested their lives to see men and women unite in ministry. While much progress has been made since their day, we still have work to do. We have yet to see Christ's body flowing together in a gift-based, no longer gender-biased, environment. Paul's declaration that "every member has been given divine gifts to contribute to the growth of all"[1] has yet to be completely realized. When that happens, we will be the fully-orbed expression of Jesus that we're called to be.

Presently there are many champions following in Anne and Jarena's footsteps. These valiant warriors are unashamed of the Gospel and unafraid of opposition. Though there are so many who could be mentioned here, I'd like to focus on a few whose hearts reflect a growing company of fearless ones. Despite their diverse situations, they represent a common trend. Increasingly, women and men are leading shared ministries as we share Good News with the world.

BETH MOORE
EVANGELIST, AUTHOR, AND BIBLE TEACHER
FOUNDER OF LIVING PROOF MINISTRIES
HOUSTON, TEXAS

Although I have never met Beth Moore personally, her ministry has touched me profoundly. Beth is the founder of Living Proof Ministries, a ministry to women. Based in Houston, Texas, she focuses on teaching women to fully experience their relationship with Jesus. Honoring the complementarian convictions of her theological stream, Beth predominantly teaches in settings attended by women. Yet I, like many other men, have also benefitted greatly from her teaching gift. She's insightful, inspiring, and articulate in her presentation of how God's Word can be applied to everyday life.

Yet Beth has experienced resistance in her desire to fulfill the call of Jesus on her life. Her right to teach has been challenged. Her motives have been questioned. And her sense of comradery with brothers in ministry has often been tentative. Until recently, she carried that burden inwardly, while pursuing her God-given destiny. To the public eye, her warm and winsome demeanor never betrayed the wounding of her heart. A friend encouraged her to put into words the pain she endured at the mistreatment of her brothers. With her permission, I include the full transcript of her blog post entitled "A Letter to My Brothers."[2]

Dear Brothers in Christ,

A few years ago, I told my friend, Ed Stetzer, that, whenever he hears the news that I'm on my deathbed, he's to elbow his way through the family members to interview me about what it's been like to be a female leader in the conservative Evangelical world. He responded, "Why can't I do that before then?"

"Because you know good and well what will happen," I answered, "I'll get fried like a chicken." After recent events following on the heels of a harrowing eighteen months, I've decided fried chicken doesn't sound so bad.

I have been a professing Evangelical for decades and, at least in my sliver of that world, a conservative one. I was a cradle role Southern Baptist by denomination with an interdenominational ministry. I walked the aisle to receive Christ as my Savior at 9 years old in an SBC church and exactly nine years later walked the aisle in another SBC church to surrender to a vocational calling. Being a woman called to leadership within and simultaneously beyond those walls was complicated to say the least but I worked within the system. After all, I had no personal aspirations to preach nor was it my aim to teach men. If men showed up in my class, I did not throw them out. I taught. But my unwavering passion was to teach and to serve women.

I lack adequate words for my gratitude to God for the pastors and male staff members in my local churches for six decades who have shown me such love, support, grace, respect, opportunity, and often right out favor. They alongside key leaders at Lifeway and numerous brothers elsewhere have no place in a larger picture I'm about to paint for you. They have brought me joy and kept me from derailing into cynicism and chronic discouragement amid the more challenging dynamics.

As a woman leader in the conservative Evangelical world, I learned early to show constant pronounced deference—not just proper respect which I was glad to show—to male leaders and, when placed in situations to serve alongside them, to do so apologetically. I issued disclaimers ad nauseam. I wore flats instead of heels when I knew I'd be serving alongside a man of shorter stature so I wouldn't be taller than he. I've ridden elevators in hotels packed with fellow leaders who were serving at the same event and not been spoken to and, even more awkwardly, in the same vehicles where I was never acknowledged. I've been in team meetings where I was either ignored or made fun of, the latter of which I was expected to understand was all in good fun. I am a laugher. I can take jokes and make jokes. I know good fun when I'm having it and I also know when I'm being dismissed and ridiculed. I was the elephant in the room with a skirt on. I've been talked down to by male seminary students and held my tongue when I wanted to say, "Brother, I was getting up before dawn to pray and to pore over the Scriptures when you were still in your pull ups."

Some will inevitably argue that the disrespect was not over gender but over my lack of formal education but that, too, largely goes back to issues of gender. Where was a woman in my generation and denomination to get seminary training to actually teach the Scriptures? I hoped it would be an avenue for me and applied and as accepted to Southwestern Seminary in 1988. After a short time of making the trek across Houston while my kids were in school, of reading the environment and coming to the realization of what my opportunities would and would not be, I took a different route. I turned to doctrine classes and tutors, read stacks of books and did my best to learn how to use commentaries and other Bible research tools. My road was messy but it was the only reasonable avenue open to me.

Anyone out in the public eye gets pelted with criticism. It's to be expected, especially in our social media culture, and those who can't stand the heat need to get out of the kitchen. What is relevant to this discussion is that several years ago when I got publicly maligned for being a false teacher by a segment of hyper-fundamentalists based on snippets taken out of context and tied together, I inquired whether or not they'd researched any of my Bible studies to reach those conclusions over my doctrine, especially the studies in recent years. The answer was no. Why? They refused to study what a woman had taught. Meanwhile, no few emails circulated calling pastors to disallow their women to do my "heretical" studies. Exhausting. God was and is and will always be faithful. He is so sovereign and all is grace. He can put us out there and pull us back as He pleases. Ours is to keep our heads down and seek Him earnestly and serve Him humbly.

I have accepted these kinds of challenges for all of these years because they were simply a part of it and because opposition and difficulties are norms for servants of Christ. I've accepted them because I love Jesus with my whole heart and will serve Him to the death. God has worked all the challenges for good as He promises us He will and, even amid the frustrations and turmoil, I would not trade lives with a soul on the earth. Even criticism, as much as we all hate it, is used by God to bring correction, endurance, and humility and to curb our deadly addictions to the approval of man.

I accepted the peculiarities accompanying female leadership in a conservative Christian world because I chose to believe that, whether or not some of the actions and attitudes seemed godly to me, they were rooted in deep convictions based on passages from 1 Timothy 2 and 1 Corinthians 14.

Then early October 16 surfaced attitudes among some key Christian leaders that smacked of misogyny, objectification, and astonishing disesteem of women and it spread like wildfire. It was just the beginning. I came face to face with one of the most demoralizing realizations of my adult life: Scripture was not the reason for the colossal disregard and disrespect of women among many of these men. It was only the excuse. Sin was the reason. Ungodliness.

This is where I cry foul and not for my own sake. Most of my life is behind me. I do so for the sake of my gender, for the sake of our sisters in Christ and for the sake of other female leaders who will be faced with similar challenges. I do so for the sake of my brothers because Christlikeness is at stake and many of you are in positions to foster Christlikeness in your sons and in the men under your influence. The dignity with which Christ treated women in the

Gospels is fiercely beautiful and it was not conditional upon their understanding their place.

About a year ago, I had an opportunity to meet a theologian I'd long respected. I'd read virtually every book he'd written. I'd looked so forward to getting to share a meal with him and talk theology. The instant I met him, he looked me up and down, smiled approvingly and said, "You are better looking than _____." He didn't leave it blank. He filled it in with the name of another woman Bible teacher.

These examples may seem fairly benign in light of recent scandals of sexual abuse and assault coming to light, but the attitudes are growing from the same dangerously malignant root. Many women have experienced horrific abuses within the power structure of the Christian world. Being any part of shaping misogynistic attitudes, whether or not they result in criminal behaviors, is sinful and harmful and produces terrible fruit. It also paints us continually as weak-willed women and seductresses. I think I can speak for many of us when I say we are neither interested in reducing or seducing our brothers.

The irony is that many of the men who will give consideration to my concerns do not possess a whit of the misogyny coming under the spotlight. For all the times you've spoken up on our behalf and for the compassion you've shown in response to "Me too," please know you have won our love and gratitude and respect.

John Bisagno, my pastor for almost thirty years, regularly said these words, "I have most often seen that, when the people of God are presented with the facts, they do the right thing." I was raised in ministry under his optimism and, despite many challenges, have not yet recovered from it. For this reason, I write this letter with hope.

I'm asking for your increased awareness of some of the skewed attitudes many of your sisters encounter. Many churches quick to teach submission are often slow to point out that women were also among the followers of Christ (Luke 8), that the first recorded word out of His resurrected mouth was "woman" (John 20:15), and that same woman was the first evangelist. Many churches wholly devoted to teaching the household codes are slow to also point out the numerous women with whom the Apostle Paul served and for whom he possessed obvious esteem. We are fully capable of grappling with the tension the two spectrums create and we must if we're truly devoted to the whole counsel of God's Word.

Finally, I'm asking that you would simply have no tolerance for misogyny and dismissiveness toward women in your sphere of influence. I'm asking for your deliberate and clearly conveyed influence toward the imitation of Christ in His attitude and actions toward women. I'm also asking for forgiveness both from my sisters and my brothers. My acquiescence and silence made me complicit in perpetuating an atmosphere in which a damaging relational dynamic has flourished. I want to be a good sister to both genders. Every paragraph in this letter is toward that goal.

I am grateful for the privilege to be heard. I long for the day—have asked for the day—when we can sit in roundtable discussions to consider ways we might best serve and glorify Christ as the family of God, deeply committed to the authority of the Word of God and to the imitation of Christ. I am honored to call many of you friends and deeply thankful to you for your devotion to Christ. I see Him so often in many of you.

In His great name,
Beth

BRIAN AND KIM ZIMMERMAN
CO-FOUNDERS OF CITY GATE MINISTRIES
LANCASTER, PA

The husband and wife team of Brian and Kim Zimmerman are known by many as true shepherds who lead with servants' hearts. City Gate is a house of prayer and a practical-needs ministry center, which is an extension of the church families that Kim and Brian co-pastor. Their partnership in ministry is as unique as their individual gift-mixes. Watching them lead, they seem to flow together seamlessly. However, their pathway has not always been easy. I spoke with them recently, and these are some excerpts from our conversation:

Tell me about your process as a couple. How did you come to be comfortable with your gifts, your leadership callings, and flowing together?

> KIM: I never felt uncomfortable with my teaching gift, as a woman. But I shrank back from using (my gift) because I saw other women step out in a way that seemed rebellious; and I didn't want to be a part of that. Then, on the other hand, I got the message from male leaders in the church that I can only do so much; that I have to be in this box.

> BRIAN: Early in our marriage, God was healing me from hurts I had as a teenager that caused me to make judgments about strong women. In the first few years of our marriage, He started to show me the call He had on Kim's life. He said, "You're called to be her husband. You're called to love and serve her. That means not holding her back. In fact, you're to get out of the way and let Me do what I want to do in her and release her to do and be everything I want her to be." I knew that God had His hand on her for something

specific, and that I was brought alongside her, and that we would walk it out together. It wasn't until the last 12 years that we started to work together in leadership within the church.

KIM: In our early years of marriage, I was the worship leader at a church. Brian was actually on the team, under my leadership.

BRIAN: I learned, and got to show other members of the team, what it was like to be her husband, but yet serve her by being part of the team. Everybody saw that it worked, that it flowed.

KIM: Yet, it was clear in that church that for women, there was a ceiling. The message was, "You can lead worship, but not teach." When I did share my thoughts and insights as I was studying, I was told I needed to get a degree, or take a homiletics class. I had my husband encouraging me, but from the leadership I felt held back.

BRIAN: At that time, I was an elder in the church. So, I was walking in a role of submitting to Kim's authority as my worship leader, but yet having authority as an elder in the church. In a very real sense, we were submitted to one another!

KIM: We were comfortable with who we were. But many other leaders over us were not. On different occasions Brian was asked to teach on a Sunday morning and Brian would say, "I can, but my wife is the one with the teaching gift, and she should be teaching." But I was never given the opportunity to teach—to use my gift—other than leading worship.

What would you say to women and men who are facing similar situations in their churches?

KIM: I would tell women who have teaching and leadership gifts to walk in humility. Know who you are. Just serve the body of Christ. Some women push for position, trying to break the glass ceiling. I told a woman just the other day, "As you're breaking the ceiling, don't forget shattered glass is falling beneath you. So, be very careful of the way you break the ceiling."

BRIAN: What I had to process as a man was not feeling threatened by a strong woman. I have a strong wife, with leadership in her. God has gifted her with it. And she has a strong teaching gift. I had to refuse to be threatened by that or feel fearful of seeing her move out and step into her calling.

And now you are co-pastors! How does that work for you, as a husband and a wife? As a man and a woman?

BRIAN: Kim knows my heart as a pastor and my gifts. She has full freedom to teach, to use the gifts that are in her. For me, to balance husband and wife, man and woman, working together—it really means seeing and understanding how our spouse is created. Knowing the purposes God has for her. It also means not being fearful of that. It means saying, "How can I serve you to be the best that you can be in what He's called you to do?" Then championing that in her and lifting her up. There's an honoring and a serving that goes both ways. Kim does the same for me. It never becomes a power struggle. It's about helping the other one to walk into the fullness of what God has for them.

KIM: I need Brian's strength to stand and do what God's calling me to do. It's loving and it's honoring of each other. We get a lot of support and encouragement from our spiritual fathers and mothers. One of our spiritual fathers recently said, "You don't fully understand that how you two function together in the body of Christ is not seen much." We started to really ponder this, because we feel like this is just who we are. This is just how we function.

BRIAN: There are things that I'm weak in, and she's strong in, and vise versa. It's all about me seeing her giftings, her seeing my giftings, and weaving them together for our call.

KIM: Brian knows I can make quick decisions when we need to. But when we need to process something, that's Brian's strength. We're learning to value each other's perspectives and move together in leading and decision-making.

BRIAN: Women bring a perspective to leadership that I won't ever have as a man. It balances everything out as we lead together, pastor together. Even when we marry a young couple, we do all the counseling and the wedding ceremony together. As husband and wife, and as pastors.

KIM: Now everyone wants both of us to marry them! But how special to have a married couple who are pastors, officiate weddings!

BRIAN: The last couple of years, we've really taken to heart that what we have is definitely something that we want to impart to others. Something powerful happens when men and women work together!

KATHERINE AND TOM RUONALA AND DANIEL ZELLI
CO-LEADERS OF GLORY CITY CHURCH
BRISBANE, AUSTRALIA

Katherine and Tom Ruonala and Daniel Zelli have been a part of a wonderful leadership team to the Glory City Church and its growing network of global churches. Katherine and her husband Tom Ruonala are the founders of Glory City Church. They've been married since 1991. Daniel and his wife Jeanice Zelli have been married since 1992. In its early years, Katherine served as the sole senior pastor of Glory

City. Daniel and his wife, Jeanice, connected with Katherine and Tom and the church several years later. After a season of prayer, honest dialogue, and preparation, Daniel joined with Katherine and Tom's co-leadership. Though it was a three-part partnership, Katherine and Daniel were the upfront leaders in the church. Within this co-leader team, Katherine retained the role of senior leader. In many ways, Daniel and Katherine became a modern-day Deborah and Barak—synergizing their gifts to further advance the church and its mission. Katherine and Daniel were able to create a greater impact for the Kingdom as they brought different strengths to the team, and exercised them in a mutually-honoring way.

The dialogue chronicled here reflects their ministry model at the time of this writing. Sometime after the interview, Daniel matured his role to include more international ministry, reducing his ability to work closely with Katherine and Tom in the day-to-day operation of the church. Just as there are changing seasons in relationships, ministry teams can come together for various lengths of time to accomplish specific purposes. Though Daniel has broadened his sphere of ministry, they continue to work together out of the same local church.

Here are some insightful moments from my earlier discussion with Katherine, her husband Tom, and Daniel:

(To Katherine) As a woman leading in the church, what advice would you give to other women called to leadership roles in the church?

KATHERINE: Women have to lead like women. If a woman is leading like a man, you might as well have a man. The benefit of a woman in church leadership is that she is a woman. She leads like a woman. She thinks like a woman. She must respect who she is. And she must respect men for who they are.

TOM: That's Katherine's hidden key. That's why she's received so well as a woman. Because she's authentically who she is.

KATHERINE: My pastor, who raised me, used to tell me, "Katherine, we like you like a woman. We like you preaching like a woman. Don't feel like you've got to preach like a man. You don't have to fit into a man's world. We want you to be who you are!" I feel like I'm part of a transitional generation. As we are culturally transitioning to women and men in leadership in the church, the next generation isn't going to have the same issues we've had to work through.

TOM: As we're culturally transitioning, it's really important that husbands who have wives called to lead in the church understand how to release and empower their wives.

KATHERINE: Tom, for me, is just so amazing. He's very confident in himself. He doesn't have any need or desire to be up front in the spotlight. He celebrates when he sees a miracle. He cheers when he sees me get a promotion. He'll tear up with joy at what the Lord's doing. He supports me. He encourages me. At home, he's still my husband, and we submit to each other in mutual submission. I submit to his protecting gift and he submits to my sensitive prophetic gift. We're learning how to support each other as a married couple first.

TOM: We know lots of women who are frustrated because the church has told husbands that they need to control their wives. The church needs to be able to teach husbands how to release their wives. To treat women like sisters in Christ. To ask, "What would Jesus have us do? And how can we empower each other?"

KATHERINE: When a man empowers his wife, it doesn't take away from him, or his manhood.

TOM: The next level of that is having husbands release their wives to work with other men. And having wives release their husbands to work with other women.

How has the co-leadership (between Katherine and Daniel) worked among the three of you?

KATHERINE: Tom and I were believing for God to supply the missing piece to our leadership. Daniel was an answer to our prayers. He brings his piece to our visioning. He thinks globally. He's got the ability to build. To make dreams realities. By working in joint leadership, we're actually able to do something. It's a very unique situation.

DANIEL: Early on we had some issues to work out. The people familiar with Glory City were used to dealing with Katherine. It limited my ability to network, to connect, to speak into a situation, or to receive input.

KATHERINE: When we were able to introduce Daniel as our co-leader, then suddenly he was included in the conversations. Then we had the capacity to be able to communicate and strategize together. For example, Daniel has his leadership gifting. It's huge. He's got so much wisdom in change management...he coaches me on leadership. I submit to that wisdom because he flourishes in a leadership environment. Even though I'm in senior leadership in the church, Tom and I are mutually submitted to one another in our marriage. I believe he has been given the gift to protect me. I trust his wisdom and discernment. If Tom says, "Hmm, I don't feel comfortable about this," I've learned to trust that he sees something, and we need to go slow.

Given the unique dynamic of your leadership model, I'm sure you've had some obstacles to overcome along the way?

DANIEL: Yes, we've had some hurdles. There will always be hurdles in any honest, healthy leadership team. Katherine is very trusting. It's one of her strengths. She's very welcoming. It draws people in. I, on the other hand, am a little more cautious. I may have a few more questions about a situation or the people involved in the situation. It's not that either one of us is right or wrong. We're learning to contribute both of our perspectives to the discernment process.

KATHERINE: The way men and women think is quite different. The way I pastor is so relational. I'm quick to say, "Let's all have a meal" or "Let's have a cup of tea together." And if someone starts telling me their dream, I'm like, "Yes! This is awesome!" Mothers want their people to do really well. But, you also need fathers who aren't going to say "Yes" to everything. Fathers who will ask, "Have you thought of this, and this, and this?" That's where Tom and Daniel are so good. Just like a father and mother work in a family, I think the same thing happens in leadership.

DANIEL: In our leadership model, there's Katherine and Tom and me. It's not just Katherine and me. But up front of the church, it's Katherine and me. One of the things I've found in working with my own wife is that we've got different levels of leadership. My wife (Jeanice) is an introvert. She thrives in her mercy gift. She'd rather serve at the table than stand up front. She'd much rather be behind the scenes. My leadership gift is able to flourish with Katherine. I'm married to my wife. She brings balance to my life. She's the right person for me. By not forcing her to be someone she's not has allowed me to be who I am. Co-leadership of a married husband and wife has its own issues. They can take their home life, even strains in their marital relationship, and allow that to be transported to the church. Because Katherine and I aren't married (to each other), we don't have any marital issues that we bring into the church. It's purely a ministry partnership.

KATHERINE: Even though Tom's not very keen about getting up front, I talk about him a lot. I talk about him when I travel, so people don't get the idea that I'm single. My pastor taught me to do this, so people don't get the false idea that I'm a raging feminist who's run off and left her family!

DANIEL: Bringing honor to our spouses and honor to our marriages is so important. It also helps when we're ministering together, so people don't think we're married (to each other).

KATHERINE: Any time we travel, Tom is usually with us. If not, there is always a third party.

DANIEL: It's just important, even for appearances. I think it's very wise.

How would you describe your leadership styles to someone new to the co-leader model?

DANIEL: We are parental. Healthy parents want their kids to fly. They live to create a legacy. If you don't have a legacy, you don't have continuation.

TOM: When Jesus said, "Ask the Father to send laborers," the word for "laborers" in the Latin Vulgate is "patrare." It means "fathers and mothers who raise and release children." Jesus was saying, "Ask the Father to send forth mothers and fathers." When you start to see this, it jumps out all over the Bible. God has always wanted men and women, mothers and fathers, leading together in the world.

KATHERINE: That's a significant revelation! That's our hope—to see both men and women working together!

DANIEL: Generally, men are just very focused. "Let's get to the solution." But women are thinking more relationally. They're usually thinking,

"How's this going to affect this and this and that and that?"

KATHERINE: Women understand women. Usually more than half of the members in a local church are women. If you don't have any leaders who are women, how are you going to figure things out?

Functioning as parents, have you ever found the people acting like kids, playing mom against dad?

KATHERINE: (Laughter) All the time! It took us a while to realize this. That's why we want to have our giftings working together so that we have a really strong, balanced leadership. It's been a work in progress!

DANIEL: Consider this, Katherine's led the church as a senior leader for nine years. Because our co-leadership is only just recent, there have been a lot of adjustments. We took an entire year, the four of us, to talk and pray and weigh the cost before doing this (establishing our co-leadership).

KATHERINE: But the benefits have been so huge for us. It's really relieved a lot of pressure. I haven't abdicated my role, but it's been such a blessing to be able to have this missing piece take us to the next level of growth and even global influence. We've seen the benefit of two putting ten thousand to flight. It's so much like

Deborah and Barak. That's basically what's happening here.

DANIEL: We've all had to make adjustments. Katherine was the senior leader for quite some time. And I'm a natural leader, so I would just normally lead.

KATHERINE: You've only ever been a senior leader!

DANIEL: Which has been a massive adjustment for me. I'm still reconciling that as we speak. But Katherine also has had to do the same. We both honor the adjustments we've both had to make. So, there's a healthy respect and a mutual humility. I was upset with something this week and Katherine said, "You've got to tell me. Otherwise how do I know?" And so that changed my attitude and then I was able to talk it through and no problem. It's all about adjustments.

KATHERINE: Communication is the key. It's the absolute key.

DANIEL: Every Monday we meet for at least two hours.

KATHERINE: He has a list, and I have a list.

DANIEL: You've got to really work at communication all the time. Keeping short accounts. And not letting anything fester.

DR. KIM MAAS
FOUNDER OF KIM MAAS MINISTRIES, INC.
FOUNDER/DIRECTOR OF WOMEN OF OUR TIME
MOORPARK, CA

Dr. Kim Maas is a dynamic prophetic teacher, speaker, and author. Her 22-year career as a registered nurse took a dramatic turn after a life-changing encounter with the Holy Spirit in 1994. In response to the fresh call of Jesus on her life, she served as a pastor in a local church for over 12 years before transitioning into her present itinerant ministry. She now travels globally, preaching and inspiring people to fulfill the call of God on their lives. Kim articulates her motivation for ministry with these words, "God is moving on the earth, through all his people, not a single denomination. All have something to contribute. All are needed in this hour." She and her husband Mike, a professional firefighter, reside in Moorpark, California.

I spoke with Kim the other day. Here are some highlights from our chat:

When did you first realize the Lord was calling you to serve as a spiritual leader, a pastor, and a prophetic teacher?

KIM: When I first received my calling, it was quite a shock to me. I never thought that it was even a possibility. I grew up in a Southern Baptist church, so it was never held out to me that as a woman I could be a minister or a leader in the church in any form or fashion. I never saw women ministers in the church. I saw women singers and worship leaders, but I never saw women behind the pulpit.

I was a mom with three little kids. I was a full-time labor and delivery nurse at a local hospital. I loved my job. I thought that was my calling. I never had any designs on being a preacher or a prophet, so I had a lot of learning to do.

I became voraciously hungry for the Word of God. God began to show me that He was going to send me around the world to teach and preach and prophesy. I didn't really know how that would possibly come about.

Did you have any role models of women teaching, traveling, and speaking?

KIM: No, not really. I was having a lot of encounters with the Holy Spirit. I was hearing God's voice. On my days off, when my kids were at school, I would spend hours in prayer and intercession. I was receiving revelation. I was having encounters with the presence of God. But there wasn't anyone who could really mentor me.

A few years later, I went to see Cindy Jacobs at a conference at a nearby church. That's when I realized, "Oh, that's what I'm like!" She became my first role model. I began to read all of her books and go to see her when she was in the area. It was as if I was being mentored from a distance.

After a series of encounters with the Lord, I realized that I couldn't get away from His call on my life. I was all the way in, completely sold out, and passionate about what He desired to do through my life.

How did your husband respond to all that was happening in you?

KIM: Prior to this, we were both going to work for 30 years, retire, and go on vacation for the rest of our lives. Mike was a leader in the fire department, but he never felt a call to ministry. He had no desire to preach or teach. Frankly, what was happening in me was scary to him. He was very oppositional in the beginning. Not because he was mean or didn't love me. It was because he didn't have the same encounters that I had. This was very, very difficult for both of us.

Then the Lord reminded me of the story of Mary and Joseph in Matthew 1. When Mary became pregnant with Jesus, Joseph struggled to understand. He wanted to put Mary away. But God came to him in a dream and said, "No, this is from Me." I knew that God was saying that I would have to wait until the moment when God speaks to my husband and shows him that my call is from the Lord. I didn't realize that it was going to take years for that to happen!

Years later, Mike had an encounter with the Holy Spirit. After God spoke to him, he said to me, "Now I really understand. You have to do this. And you have to do this for the rest of your life. And I'm going to be with you in this, to do this." It shifted everything in that moment, in a brand-new way.

But until that time, I had to walk in obedience to the Lord, feeling like I was in opposition to some of the things I had been taught as a woman in the church. I know I'm not the only woman who has felt that way. The struggle in my heart was very painful. I kept saying, "Lord, I don't want to do anything that hurts the church, hurts Your name, is in opposition to Your Word."

What did you do between the time of your calling and the time of your husband's confirming encounter with the Lord?

KIM: The Lord kept saying to me, "Go to seminary." I resisted for a while, until He said, "If you do not go, you are in disobedience to Me, and obedience to Me comes before obedience to your husband." The Lord essentially told me that my husband loves me enough and is for me enough that, even if he doesn't understand what I'm doing, he would continue to move forward as I move forward. That I would just have to remain obedient to the Lord, even if it seemed like I was in disobedience to my husband.

What were your next steps?

KIM: I became a full-time pastor on the leadership staff at a local Foursquare church. I also went to seminary for four years, and for four years I was stigmatized and faced opposition in many ways. On my first day of seminary, I turned on a Christian radio station as I drove the 45-minute drive to school. Immediately, I heard a radio preacher say that he felt the doctrine of women in ministry in the church was a doctrine of demons. I felt like I had been pierced in my heart. It hit me like a dart from the enemy, and I fell apart in my car, sobbing. I hadn't worked out my theology yet regarding women in ministry.

When I arrived at the school, I went straight to my seminary counselor's office. After telling him my dilemma, he said, "There are several views regarding women in ministry. What you heard today is just one of them." He continued, "I'm going to tell you this. I can't work out your theology for you." He said, "You're going to have to land on a theological position you feel is biblically supported so that you know that you can do what you're called to do."

So, I enrolled in a class studying the issue of women in ministry. I learned all the various views, then I had to find my own place to stand. As women called to ministry, we all have to find our place to stand. There are going to be various views in the church. And when you go to minister, there are going to be people who vehemently disagree with you and call you all kinds of names, like an unsubmitted woman or a Jezebel.

How did you learn to continue in the face of opposition?

KIM: Two very pivotal things happened. First, I learned to hear the voice of God. Then, I learned the biblical foundation for women in ministry. Those two things helped me find a place to stand so that I could withstand any of the opposition I would face.

What would you say to young women who are being called into ministry?

KIM: I would say, "Now is your time. Now is your time." Be fearless. Do everything God has asked you to do. Leave nothing out. Pursue God with everything that you are. And when the time comes for you to think about dating and getting married, make sure that from the very beginning, that young man understands that you have a call of God on your life. That you intend to do everything God asks you to do without condition. And that you want him to be by your side and you want him to come with you. That you will support his call and the gifts in his life. That you will encourage him and his call and his gifts, just as vehemently as you pursue your own call.

Pursuing the call of God doesn't mean that you can't have a family. It doesn't mean you can't be a mother and a grandmother and a wife. Because in those seasons of your life as a woman, you will modify how you pursue the call. And God will show you how to modify that so that your children, your husband, your grandchildren, have your time and your investment and know you as a person. So that they feel connected with you in all the ways that they should. You can have those roles and that influence in their lives, yet still continue to follow the call on your life.

Being a mother is a role and an assignment. Serving in the church is a role and an assignment. Going on the mission field is a role and an assignment. But your identity is actually as a son of God, because sons are both male and female, just like being the Bride of Christ is both male and female.

Your identity is as a son of God. But the assignments will change. They will morph, as you fulfill them. I have watched women who see their role as a mother as their identity. I have seen these women pour their lives into their children, yet they don't continue to develop themselves as a person separate from their children. You want to continue to grow and develop in your personal life, separate from your role as a wife, separate from your role as a minister, separate from your role as a mother. So that whatever assignment you're called into, you're ready to fulfill that assignment.

EILEEN VINCENT
CO-FOUNDER OF OUTPOURING MINISTRIES
PROPHETIC TEACHER, AUTHOR
FOUNDER OF CITY REACHERS:
FOR THE LOVE OF SAN ANTONIO
SAN ANTONIO, TX

Eileen Vincent and her husband, Alan, are powerful Bible teachers, missionary pioneers, and spiritual leaders, each in their own right. Since their life-changing encounters with the Lord in the late 1950s, they've been blazing a trail of revival throughout India, Africa, Europe, and the United States. Their teachings are thoroughly inspiring and profoundly insightful. Not only has their message made an impact, but their example of shared ministry has inspired many gifted women to co-labor with their brothers. Together, the Vincent's have pressed through seasons of being misunderstood and marginalized because of their ministry partnership. Yet many people consider them to be spiritual parents who have laid wise foundations. My wife and I are among that company of grateful daughters and sons.

In recent years Alan's strong voice was tragically silenced, the result of a harrowing battle with dementia. During this trying period, Eileen remained a constant source of strength and encouragement to her beloved husband. Alan passed on April 8, 2020, entering into the glorious presence of the Lord and leaving a wonderful, world-changing legacy. His was a life well-lived!

Eileen continues to be a strong maternal influence in the family of God. Shortly before Alan's death, I had the privilege of spending some time with her. Even in her 80s, Eileen perpetually exudes a childlike wonder and youthful spunk. She leads City Reachers, a prayer and outreach ministry in her home town of San Antonio. In addition, her plucky preaching still inspires crowds of spiritually hungry people of all ages. Here are some significant moments from our conversation.

Eileen, you are among some of the bravest, most passionate people I know. When did all of this start?

EILEEN: I grew up as a person who was utterly determined. When I look back, I probably would have been called stubborn. When I came to Christ, it was so radical—so utterly radical. I was just going to serve God with every conceivable thing I had. When I was seven years old, my sister remembers me coming out of Sunday School saying, "I'm going to be a missionary when I grow up!"

Then I got married and really came to the Lord. And when I really got converted, I said to Alan, my husband, "Okay, now we've got to go! We're going to be missionaries." And he said, "What? Where?"

People used to call me a trailblazer. Throughout our married life, I would open the way for Alan to go and preach. I was the first one to go to South Africa. I opened the way and then everybody loved Alan's preaching. He would like me to go and do what I do. And I loved it, too. I would make connections, open the doors, take the platform, encourage the people, and open the way. It's worked so well for us through the years.

After South Africa, off we went to India. In some ways, women in a missions situation can feel a bit freer to be themselves. So I took advantage of the freedom to be myself. Alan was in full agreement. Alan is a very incredible man of God with an amazing gifting and also a strong leader. I am also a leader. So here we were—a couple of strong leaders. We were a household of generals. So you can imagine it was not always peace. But never boring.

How were you received in church settings as a strong leader *and* a woman?

EILEEN: Shortly after we arrived in India, the pastor of our church took Alan aside and said, "You've got to deal with your wife and take control. She must be quiet." As we later discovered, they objected to the fact that I could initiate an idea. The male leaders expected their wives to just do what they were told. The fact that I could initiate something was a problem for them. These men seemed tremendously insecure.

How did that impact you?

EILEEN: I came to absolutely hate myself over all of this. I thought, "God, I've just got to be a different person." I remember picking out a very quiet woman in our church, and saying, "If only I could be like her. She's so sweet. She doesn't offend anybody." I went through so many awful things in my own mind trying to be like somebody else. Then I realized, after a lot of dealings with the Lord, that the anointing of the Lord upon some people can be intimidating to other people.

Did the opposition you've felt primarily come from men, or from women, or from both?

EILEEN: In India, it was primarily men. But when we came home to church-plant in England, both men and women came after me there. Alan became part of an apostolic team which was part of the shepherding movement that had a very restrictive attitude toward women in ministry. I was allowed to share my prophetic gift, because they consented that the scriptures support women prophesying. But when I passionately taught the Word, I was confronted immediately by the leaders. I was told, "You were raising your voice. A woman may share, but she may never preach." Women were forced to wear head coverings. We were encouraged to carry ourselves in a diminutive way.

I was constantly getting in trouble with the leaders because of my preaching style. I felt bruised. It was enough to make anybody want to give up, and many women did. But I didn't.

I had battled with and been beaten down by both men and women in the church. All of our elders were men. Some of their wives had no ministry leadership giftings whatsoever. They were the women who came at me. My gifting and calling were foreign to them. They just couldn't relate to me. Those husbands and those wives were the most vocal.

Was it a matter of their biblical convictions, or was it personal?

EILEEN: I think they felt they had a biblical conviction. They pointed to a few passages and told me to submit to my husband and keep silent in the church. Then one day I found a book that gave fresh exposition on those difficult passages in 1 Timothy and 1 Corinthians. So I did a very careful, careful study. I researched from every angle. I had mega questions. I asked the Lord to give me clear answers. I eventually came to peace as I found clear answers to my questions. I knew that I was standing on solid rock ground.

We became so convinced, Alan and I started to teach it [biblical support about men and women leading and ministering together]. We taught with deep sensitivity, remembering our own journey. You have so many fears because, in your heart of hearts, you don't want to be out of order.

Was there a significant event that caused a turning point in your life and ministry?

EILEEN: Things miraculously came to a turning point after I returned from Seoul, South Korea. I was researching my book, *God Can Do It Here*, by studying Dr. Paul Yonggi Cho's huge church. I went alone, and I was there for just about a month. When I came home, Alan wanted to hear everything that happened. Cho had laid his hands on me and prayed for me. Alan knew that something had happened to me—that the power of God was upon me.

The next day, Alan was scheduled to preach at a large meeting in the city of Bath. The apostolic network he was a part of had organized the event. As we were driving there, Alan kept saying to me, "I haven't got the word, but you do!" But I thought, how on earth could I speak at such a meeting? It was too imposing a situation. The whole apostolic team were there, sitting on the platform, and I was allowed to sit next to Alan on the end. I got to sit there because Alan told them, "Eileen just returned from Dr. Paul Yonggi Cho's church, and she's got something to say." After a lot of deliberation, they said, "She can share just a few minutes." And so, I was given the platform, but I was incredibly uncomfortable. All the men were sitting behind me in a row. As I walked forward, I felt all their eyes were sort of burning holes in me.

The Spirit of the Lord came upon me, and I began to preach. I certainly was longer than a few moments. I was feeling, "Oh God, what on earth do I do?" But the power of God was present, and the people were responding, and no one was telling me to be quiet or to step down. And so, I continued. As soon as I was finished, I left the building and went and sat in the car.

I was so frightened. I just kept saying, "I've crossed the line! I've crossed the line!" I crossed the invisible line where no woman should ever go. I was usurping the place of the men. I felt so devastated. My devastation went on for about three days. I was in a terrible place of despair. Then I had an extremely strange experience.

The Spirit of the Lord came to me. It was as if God invited me into His very presence, as He put out a red carpet. I remember feeling absolutely intimidated, almost terrified. But the Lord was inviting me to come. I stepped onto that red carpet, and He said to me, "Eileen, the gift, the anointing, the calling, and the ministry do not belong to the men, but they belong to Me. Steward them for Me." And then He repeated it, "The gift, the anointing, the calling, and the ministry do not belong to the men, but they belong to Me. Steward them for Me." And that was it. In that moment, I was delivered from the fear of men, just by the awesome fear of God. And I tell you, although situations never changed from that point on [within the organization], my root attitude was radically changed. I knew that if I walked carefully and humbly before my God, if my attitudes were right, if I sought to obey God—even if certain men had problems with who I am and who I'm called to be—that was their problem, and not mine. I wasn't going to take the guilt of it any more. And so, that was a mega-amazing turning point in my whole life.

What would you say to women who have leadership gifts, yet they are in systems where they are not free to use their gifts?

EILEEN: First of all, seek God Himself. Seek to know and represent His heart. Our greatest calling is to represent Christ. We are not card-waving, angry women demanding our freedom, our liberty, our rights. We want to be the best, purest representation of Christ Himself. Go after God—deeply after His heart. That's your starting place. He will purify your motives there. He'll also purify your gift.

Also, if you're married, appreciate your husband's position. My husband was on a journey also. On top of that, he had a wife who was not fitting the mold of a "proper church woman." He was part of an apostolic group of men who had different ideas [about women] and he became the misfit of that group. In the end, Alan was put out of the group because he decided to stand with me. He actually preached against head coverings before that organization got rid of them!

I am grateful to the Lord for Alan. I am so grateful for the opportunities I've had to use my gifts for the Lord's glory. We must release women to join with men in serving the Lord. How can over half of the church be irrelevant and unemployed? Just to sit there and receive, instead of doing? Not being permitted to take up the commission of Christ and do His works? My heart would be aching if I didn't get to do the things I've been blessed to be able to do!

CHAPTER 12

OUR STORY

"Every time there has been a spiritual awakening, women are often called up into ministry and spiritual leadership. It's one of the signs of a revival that isn't talked about very often."

–Kadi Cole

WOMEN AND MEN LEAD DIFFERENTLY. BUT TOGETHER, THEY LEAD SIGNIFICANTLY BETTER!

To think that one day I would make such a statement is personally astounding!

I grew up in a church culture where the thought of men and women leading together never seemed to be a consideration. Yet through the years, I had an increasing sense that a grave injustice had been done—that a wrong needed to be righted. The biblical and social concerns addressed in this book are ones I've been challenged by, frustrated with, and even afraid of. I've ignored them, trivialized them, and marginalized them—until encountering God's heart about them.

That changed everything for me!

The journey has been challenging—and something I haven't taken lightly. I've researched, pondered, prayed about, and pressed through these issues until they've become more than "issues." Now they're essentials. It's essential that the entire team gets to play. It's vital that every man and every woman gets to utilize their gifts and fulfill their God-given callings. We need the whole army to win this war.

As a pastor who was leading an all-male pastoral team and an all-male eldership, the absence of women on our leadership teams became increasingly noticeable. For me, it was the proverbial elephant in the boardroom. Not every leader felt this way. My initial attempts at broaching the subject were met with either patronizing nods or blank stares. Eventually, they spoke up. Some diminished its importance, saying, "Dave, we have lots of areas needing our attention. Are you sure this is something God wants us to deal with now?" Others expressed concerns about the impact on the church, cautioning, "Not everyone's going to agree with this. We could lose some people." A few spoke from their deep convictions and personal interpretations of Scripture, expressing, "I see what the Bible clearly says. I just can't get around that. Women should not exercise any authority in the church." Still others warned, "If we adjust our position based on a fresh interpretation of God's Word, what other convictions will we concede? Will we eventually compromise our stance on our moral values?" Every one of these concerns was valid, and worth considering. Needless to say, we had a lot of work ahead of us.

Initially, the leaders whose wives have strong teaching and leadership gifts understood the struggle many women in the church face. They had seen their spouses kept out of places that could benefit from their contributions. Meanwhile, other elders had wives who avoided the limelight and had no desire to serve with men in leadership capacities. With their gifts such as mercy, hospitality, and helps, they felt joy and fulfillment serving in lesser-seen areas. But then something happened—seemingly a Holy Spirit "set-up"—that caught all of our attention.

As an eldership, we were processing a particularly difficult issue, completely unrelated to the subject of women in leadership. After prolonged discussions and seasons of prayer, we were still unable to come to consensus. Finally, during one exasperating debate, we committed to spend the next seven days in focused prayer on the topic. When we reconvened, the group was amazed to find that we came into agreement almost immediately. One by one, each elder shared what the Lord had shown him during the week of prayer. Grins spanned the table as we enjoyed the peace and clarity the Father's wisdom had brought to us. Then, one elder made a confession. He sheepishly admitted that he and his wife had prayed together about the issue at hand. During their joint time of intercession, his wife received the revelation he had shared with us that night. Immediately, another elder told a similar story.

Before long, every elder around the table confessed that while the Lord had truly spoken to him, in each case, His voice sounded a lot like his wife's voice! Almost without hesitation, one of the elders who had been most resistant to processing the issue of women in leadership suggested that we look into it. And so, we began.

THE JOURNEY BEGINS

Our eldership team prepared to thoroughly process this matter, taking as much time as would be needed. And heading into this potentially volatile interchange, we established a few boundaries. We committed to guard the unity of the Holy Spirit among us, to share our thoughts honestly, and to listen to other perspectives, honoring one another even when we disagreed. We determined to remain teachable, noting that on this side of Heaven, we only "know in part."[1] We expressed a personal willingness to adjust our thinking and our theology to fresh revelations of truth, acknowledging the "*we*" of "*we* have the mind of Christ,"[2] meant that no singular person corners the market on all truth. Though intense at times, this season proved to be one of the most bonding experiences of my life.

Before zeroing in on the handful of epistolary passages that are commonly used to forbid women, we agreed to begin with a fresh approach to the entire Bible. What was God's original design for men and women? How has He moved in and through both genders in the course of history? Setting aside the opinions that have prevailed in the church, what is our Father's heart for His children and our shared fulfillment of His purposes?

Together, we voiced a prayer similar to David's petition in Psalm 139:24: "Lord, show us if there is any 'twisted'[3] way in our thinking. Are there mindsets that grieve You? Are we processing in ways that are based on opinion and misaligned with Your ways?" We began this journey in the latter part of 2002. With the passing of time, it's difficult for me to provide a chronological account of our discussions. However, I can clearly recollect the highlights of our processing.

As the older brother of two siblings, I recall a scenario that was frequently replayed in my childhood. In our playtimes, my younger brother and I loved to create various recreational setups. We eagerly covered the basement floor with tiny green plastic army men to reenact D-Day. We lined the backyard with powdered lime for our version of a two-man Super Bowl. Our favorite scenario included posing a battalion of 12-inch-tall G.I. Joes for the ultimate military tour. However, in the midst of our engrossing endeavors, we were often confronted with a singular roadblock to our afternoon entertainment: our sister. After we rejected her pleas to participate, the tears would flow. And then her wailing appeal to our dad would result in him insisting with fatherly authority, "Let your sister play." This inconvenient order meant we had to accommodate stuffed animals among the soldiers at Normandy. Cheerleading interrupted our game-saving touchdowns. And a barrage of Barbies domesticated our G.I. Joes. Little did I realize that a philosophy was indelibly etched in my brain: "It is not good to let girls play."

Advancing several decades to prayerfully processing this issue with my fellow elders, I recognized that a childhood prejudice was still prevalent in my thinking: "It is not good to let women play." In the early days of our biblical research, my deep-seated judgment had a direct encounter with the Word of God. Our "no girls allowed" clubhouse had a visit from the Father who said, "*It is not good for man to be alone.*"[4] I suddenly saw my predisposition in light of His revelation. Not only did my earthly father want us to let our sister play, but my Heavenly Father has always wanted His daughters and sons to unite. "Let them rule" throbs with His desire for our shared ministries to impact the planet.

Those who had cautioned me that letting women in leadership circles only serves to emasculate men, caused me to overlook a powerful truth. Women leading with men does not emasculate men, nor does men leading with women defeminize women. We weren't created to compete with one another. Our shared ministry doesn't diminish our unique identities. *Both* male and female were created in God's image to fully reflect Him. Instead of competing for supremacy, we're completing the reflected image of God on the earth. I was allowing the fear of being emasculated to detour me from our call to emulate the nature of God together.

As I shared my discovery with the rest of the elders, they also told of similar experiences. Hurts had to be healed, people had to be forgiven, and wrong thinking had to be repented of, in order for us to align our hearts with the heart of God. For some, the rite of passage into the male culture of their families included an unspoken agreement to disdain women. For others, female authority figures had to be released from bitter judgments. There were demeaning experiences with ruler-wielding teachers and shame-filled corrections from punitive female authority figures that had kept our barriers in place. Sweeping stereotypes had to be revoked. We felt corrected by our Father for punishing half the human race, labeling them as Jezebels unfit for ministry.

We also gained fresh insights into the Word of God. Like an obscure image suddenly gaining clarity, we increasingly saw both men and women in spiritual leadership in both Old and New Testaments. The early church especially reflected the collaborative ministries of both genders. Keeping a bird's-eye view of the entirety of the biblical record helped us to navigate the specific "keep silent/I forbid" passages in their context. Reflecting on those days, three factors were key highlights of our journey.

First and foremost, we devoted ourselves to prayer. Serving as leaders in the body of Christ is a sobering responsibility. We desired to follow Paul's admonition to be people who are "accurately handling the word of truth."[5] So we humbled our hearts before the Lord in a lifestyle of prayer. We prayed individually and corporately. One of our constant requests was, "Show me Your ways, Lord, teach me Your paths."[6] This was clearly not about reinforcing our fixed opinions, solidifying our biases, or accommodating our personal comfort zones. We desperately desired to know the heart of God on this matter, regardless of what it would cost us. We were prepared to align our hearts with His.

Secondly, we began to include our wives in the discussion. In hindsight, it seems ridiculous that we didn't do this from the start. But in those days, we had limited perspective on just how vital both mothers and fathers are to the health of the church family. Up to this point, we had affectionately referred to the wives of elders as "Eldorados." We thought it was mildly humorous. Later, we discovered that many of our wives found it to be deeply hurtful. Ironically, the Spanish proper name "El Dorado" denotes a place filled with abundance and opportunities. Yet for women with spiritual leadership gifts, the opportunities were far from abundant.

As our wives joined us in the discussion, we also included a single woman who was part of our church staff. She was spiritually mature, integrous, and highly gifted administratively. She gave wise and comprehensive leadership to the administration of the church, and truly pastored both our men and women. Though she served in the role of an executive pastor, she was never given the title or the authority. And while she periodically attended our elders' meetings, providing updates and insights, she was never included in the final decision-making process on this issue. One of my many regrets is that she was never fully honored for who she was and for the calling on her life.

A final highlight of this process was the discovery of the book, Why Not Women?, co-authored by Loren Cunningham and David Joel Hamilton.[7] We were familiar with Loren Cunningham, the founder of Youth With a Mission, a world-wide network of outreach ministries. His global perspectives on gender issues in ministry settings were deeply insightful. An added bonus was David Joel Hamilton's expert handling of the scriptures, reflecting both his extensive research and his thoughtful, humble heart. *Why Not Women?* gave us necessary confirmation to our interpretations of difficult biblical passages. It also stretched us to consider other perspectives in our pursuit of truth. This was only one of many resources we gleaned from. We deliberately considered input from books that were both for and against women serving in church leadership.

Many of the insights I covered in earlier chapters of this book reflect the discernments we made together during this phase of our expedition. The addition of women in the discussion caused our times to be richer and more connected. Both genders saw things with new eyes and greater understanding. As the word "understanding" implies, revelation came as we "stood under" the perspectives of one another. It's true that at times, we experienced moments of "intense fellowship" as opinions were strongly proposed on either side of an issue. Voices were raised and convictions were debated. But in the end, we sought to stand together under the wise counsel of the Wonderful Counselor.

At intervals along our journey, there were poignant moments of healing for our souls. A new transparency developed among us as we truly wrestled with issues and faced our own fears. One woman confessed that she rather enjoyed influencing the church vicariously through her husband's eldership. Yet she also acknowledged that if a decision unexpectedly failed in its results, there was relief in knowing that she hadn't directly participated in making it. A number of other women shared that they, too, had similar feelings.

Others verbalized their hesitancy to reject traditions handed to them by respected ancestors. One elder, personally paralyzed by this mindset, had a significant perspective-altering encounter with the Lord. He was reminded that his spiritual predecessors had been spiritual pioneers in their day. At a time when the grace gifts of the Holy Spirit—namely healing and prophecy—were largely refused by many churches, they too had studied the scriptures and pursued a change. Although they'd been labeled as "heretics" and worse, they championed a revolution that still has reverberating impact on the world. Reconnecting with their pioneering spirit, he resolved to embrace change, not simply for the sake of change, but for the cause of conviction. We determined to honor our predecessors, while not allowing our history to rob us of our destiny.

One elder confessed that every time he heard the phrase "women in leadership," he pictured a specific female church leader from his past who used intimidation and manipulation to get her way. As he processed this before the Lord, he saw that intimidation was not gender-exclusive. He was reminded of countless male leaders who also used force of personality to impose their will on others. He realized that we cannot forbid anyone their God-appointed leadership roles simply because others have exploited those roles. One by one, our Father brought increased clarity and healing to us in signature ways.

I'm not comfortable with "top-down" leadership styles. I hold a deep conviction that leaders don't gather simply to speak *their* minds and make decisions. Instead we come together to seek *His* mind and make discernments. For this reason, I was compelled to give ample time for everyone to pray and process the issues at hand. We had all come from different places theologically; and based on our temperaments and past experiences, we all moved at different paces, as well.

After two years of prayerful processing, we came to the settled consensus that both women and men were created by God to lead together—in the home, in the church, and in the world. We saw it in His Word. We experienced it in His heart. In November of 2007, the elders of Christ Community Church in Camp Hill, Pennsylvania officially upgraded our by-laws to welcome women to join with men in every facet of church leadership, according to their character, giftings, and callings.

Prior to announcing our new position on this issue, I shared a series of sermons covering the biblical foundations that support men and women in leadership in the church. In the ensuing months, we as pastors and elders processed the change with our members. Most of the questions people raised were identical to the concerns we had faced. Just as the elders had taken time to process, the church required the same. As with most changes in church-life, the responses were varied. Some people left the church. Others sat face-to-face with members of the leadership team, sharing heart-to-heart. Some raised questions. Others raised challenges. Most people experienced the same peace we had, as they saw that the whole of scriptural support outweighs the few, isolated verses and interpretations that are without context. This was a liberating shift in our philosophy of ministry, freeing men and women to lead side by side in our church.

On the Sunday we officially announced our open door to shared ministry and leadership between the genders, the sanctuary was filled with shouts of joy and applause. Many personally expressed their gratitude for an environment of unhindered possibilities for their children and grandchildren. They captured the reality that this was not merely a women's liberation issue. Rather, this brought freedom to all. It was a very tangible demonstration of the truth that Jesus has removed every gender, racial, and socioeconomic barrier. In Christ, there is simply no room for such limitations.

I wish that I could say every problem was resolved that day. But we have learned that while changing the by-laws is one issue, transforming the culture is another—requiring more time than amending a document. We proceeded slowly but steadily, resisting pendulum swings while seeking to simply keep in step with the Holy Spirit. Through it all, we continued to remind ourselves that people process change at different paces, and some may arrive at different conclusions from our own. The Father's love makes room for both dialogue and decisions. As we proceeded, some deepened their connections to our church family and others disconnected in order to pursue a church culture with which they felt better aligned.

Regional pastors, observing us from afar, warned that such a move would open the door to swarms of militant misandrists (i.e., those who despise men) seeking power positions. But nothing like that ever happened. Though motivations behind those aspiring to church leadership can be as varied as the individuals themselves, we discovered a consistent trend among generations of dynamically gifted women. Rather than seething with revenge over decades of exclusion, they were teeming with joy-filled boldness. For them, it wasn't an issue of women's rights. Instead it was the conviction that everyone has the right and responsibility to fulfill the call of God on their life. They have embraced their gender—not as a license nor a liability—but as a God-given component of their calling.

In the years since adding women to our leadership teams, we've experienced better stability, broader perspectives, wiser counsel, and stronger connections. Just as healthy families require the oversight of both fathers and mothers, our church family has experienced the powerful presence of both. This has been one of the most proactive steps we've ever taken to improve the quality of our leadership. And as in any cultural adjustment, we still have issues to confront and improvements to make.

THE SURVEY SAYS....

I recently surveyed or interviewed all of the leaders in our church, both men and women. I wanted to evaluate how much our climate and culture have changed since our guidelines were transformed. Though I conducted the interviews face-to-face, I also sent a blind survey, allowing for anonymity and encouraging candid responses. I was pleasantly surprised at the results.

Over half of our leaders were raised in churches where women had limited or no opportunities to be involved in ministry oversight. The same number of leaders regularly received negative input regarding women in leadership, in the form of sermons and statements from male authority figures. Yet the vast majority of those I surveyed stated that they had made significant alterations in their personal convictions. They wholeheartedly agreed that men and women must be equally released to serve and lead in any capacity. One male leader, who's been a part of our church for over 45 years, shared this perspective, "When I first came here, every leader was a man. Couples were periodically allowed to minister, but never a woman alone." He continued, "When we began to purposefully make a shift to set women in as elders and pastors, there was resistance. However, women bring something that men don't bring." He concluded, "This gives us a healthy perspective when we make decisions impacting the church as a whole. It paints a healthier picture when women are involved [in leadership]."

A female leader voiced her approval of our current practice by offering, "We are sending a clear message that we accept a person who's strong—male or female—because it's okay to be that way. It's okay to be strong. It's okay to be bold."

Other responses, however, indicated that we still have work to do. A female leader, when asked if she has experienced resistance in her leadership role, responded, "It has never been blatant. But there are subtle hints that have communicated disapproval [from other male leaders and female church members]."

Another leader shared, "I believe we've come a long way, even in the last ten years. Yet, some still frown on women as elders." One leader added, "I just think there are some older members that, no matter what we do, will not change their views at this point. I just hope we can introduce the younger members to a new culture. As we affirm the younger men and women, eventually this is going to grow, and male-dominance will be a thing of the past."

The most surprising part of the survey was the leaders' reaction to the question, "How would you describe the general response of our congregation to the increasing role of women in ministry and leadership?" Slightly less than half indicated a sense of wholehearted approval among the members of the church. However slightly more than half sensed congregational approval with some reservation toward women and men in leadership. The leaders I interviewed were not surprised by this survey result. One male leader posed this perspective, "I've seen us come a long way as a church since we first introduced the concept of women as elders—more than just a woman teaching a class, but stepping into a place of authority. I still hear infrequent comments, usually from men stuck in the male-dominant model. But it seems very infrequent." "When probed," another leader inserted, "those who are uncomfortable with men and women leading together don't seem to base it on a strong biblical perspective. I think a lot of it is merely personal perspective." Whether frequent or sporadic, widespread or localized, this survey response does reflect the fact that not all of our members are yet fully accepting of the shared ministry leadership model.

In the second-to-last survey question, I wanted to discover how collaborative ministry was working at the grassroots level. Were women and men truly learning to work together in an effective, supportive way? The overwhelming majority of leaders indicated that, in spite of periodic difficulties, progress was being made. A female leader cited, "We've experienced more clashes [on our leadership team] between task-focused and relationally-oriented individuals. Both men and women can be one or the other. Personality clashes can be more significant than conflicts between genders." She noted, "The male leaders are learning to listen longer and make eye contact." Another woman in leadership confessed, "Since stepping into a leadership role, I've moved into a more direct approach. I've moved from apologizing for my presence to learning to stand up more and be more direct. I'm learning how to lead. How to be more decisive. I needed to learn to understand others, especially men." Acknowledging the unique ways many men and women process decisions, a female leader mentioned, "You can't get offended." Rehearsing a situation where she felt marginalized because of her gender, she responded, "But I didn't for a moment back down on the gifting God had put in me." I find great encouragement in this revelation. Working together takes work! In hearing a sample of our leaders' hearts, there emerged a passionate resolve to press through obstacles in order to secure the health and wisdom of joint-leadership ventures. Two are truly better than one![8]

Of the entire evaluation, the final survey question gave me the greatest inspiration. Virtually every leader responded affirmatively to the statement: "We will continue to mature and benefit from our co-laboring." A male leader summarized, "I believe it brings the fullness of God's heart. We all contribute so much. When we come together to make connections and make decisions, it is the full heart of God. The emotion, the strategy, the different perspectives—that is a huge benefit of making sure we're all at the same table together." With the same exuberance, another expressed, "I love the culture here. I love what we're doing. It's awesome! It's liberating! It's freeing!"

When I asked one leader to share her thoughts on how we should proceed, she encouraged, "We must keep re-emphasizing the fact that we believe men and women serving together is both wise and biblical. Continue to release men and women to fully lead. We must share that it's not about gender, but about qualification and anointing and character. The more both men and women consistently speak and teach and preach and lead will only serve to reinforce this truth. It's so worth it!"

Despite obvious challenges, this corporate journey has been priceless. Even in telling you our story, my heart is stirred afresh. We have been apprehended by a God who made us as one flesh, who called us to rule together, and who poured His Spirit upon His sons and daughters to reveal His heart to the world.

This truly has been a thoroughly inspiring journey! In the words of one of our leaders, "It's so worth it!"

CHAPTER 13

YOUR STORY

"Arise, my dearest. Hurry, my darling. Come away with me! I have come as you have asked to draw you to my heart and lead you out. For now is the time, my beautiful one. The season has changed, the bondage of your barren winter has ended, and the season of hiding is over and gone."

Song of Solomon 2:10-11 (TPT)

The season is changing, and a new day is dawning. The suppression of women in the name of submission is dissipating. Gender-biased restrictions are being questioned and challenged, making room for gift-based ministry leadership in the church. No longer is this merely an issue to debate. It's now become a lifestyle to fulfill. One of our church leaders expressed her gratitude for this present reality, saying, "I so appreciate being received in leadership settings. I'm grateful to be welcomed in circles of decision-making. I'm so glad we're not just working to show that we like women. But we're working hard to demonstrate that everybody on the team matters. Both male and female."

By God's grace, we seek to establish a culture of honor for every person in our church—a climate where both genders are free to experience the love of God and express it uniquely. Together, we seek to reach our corporate potential. In these days of increasing outpourings of the Holy Spirit, it's urgent that all ages and both genders are released in His holy surge. It will take the whole body of believers, fully deployed and powerfully present, to influence the whole world with the whole Gospel.

I want to encourage you to pursue the writing of your own story. For some, our story is confirming. For others, it's challenging. Before choosing sides and drawing lines, I encourage you to prayerfully pause. The last thing I want to do is provide more fuel for yet another church fight, depleting our strength and distracting our focus. While developing a gender-inclusive leadership environment has greatly enhanced our church, it hasn't become our primary focus. Our gaze is fixed upon worshipping Jesus with abandon and seeing multitudes of people experience Him and follow Him.

MOVING FORWARD

For every person desiring to pursue this subject further or explore ways your current situation could change, I offer a few suggestions. First and foremost, closely evaluate your theological position regarding women and men in spiritual leadership. Whether you support or oppose this view, take a closer look at why. Upon what biblical foundation is your perspective based? Is it predominantly founded on a few, isolated verses, or is it consistent with overarching Scriptural themes? I encourage you to seek the Lord's counsel prayerfully—both in the Bible and while in His presence. This is the most important component in any pursuit of truth. Knowing why we believe something is almost as crucial as knowing what we believe. If we're unable to explain how we arrived at our convictions, we'll have trouble sustaining them when facing opposition.

Secondly, consider meeting with others who also feel compelled to search out the place of women in the life of the church. We found that honesty and honor were vital in our discussion groups. The book of *Proverbs* frequently refers to people who are "fools"—a term meant to be descriptive, not insulting. In this context, "fool" defines someone who's indifferent about their lifestyle, oblivious to the consequences of their choices, and resistant to input from others. One proverbial statement captures the heart of a fool by stating, "A fool delights only in revealing his or her own mind."[1] Fools always frustrate group processing. Arrogant rants and endless monologues by those who are unwilling to consider another opinion will quickly bring the quest for truth to a screeching halt. While there's no perfect way to "foolproof" your group, some healthy ground rules for establishing effective corporate discernment include agreeing to listen, asking more questions than you provide answers, and being open to receive correction.

Thirdly, take an honest assessment of the culture of your ministry family. Is your church predominantly male-friendly, female-friendly, or open and honoring to both genders? Are women passively allowed, openly resisted, or wholeheartedly embraced in leadership roles? Are there adequate opportunities and sufficient training settings for both men and women to be developed as leaders? Observe your corporate gatherings and primary leadership meetings. Are both genders equally represented, or is there an obvious bias one way or the other? In making these and other evaluations of your church culture, resist the temptation to vilify your leaders. I'm learning that all of us walk in light of the revelation we presently have. Most people, leaders included, don't sit up at night scheming new ways to make life miserable for others. Give others the benefit of the doubt. Believe the best in them, and pray for them.

Next, saturate all of your discussions and research with prayer. I don't make this statement glibly. Speaking from experience (i.e., mistakes I've made), prayer is a great way to permeate our hearts with our Father's perspective. When prayer has become a remote option, I find myself getting critical, frustrated, overwhelmed, and hopeless. Prayer does change things—primarily the heart of the one praying. Prayer doesn't instantly alter the opinions of others, and its goal isn't to coerce them. Instead, when I pray, my perspective of others becomes redemptive, because the fruit of prayer cleanses us. As you pray for your leaders, your church members, and even your opponents—Father's love for them will fill your heart. Then your prayer life will influence the lives of those around you, because you're being transformed.

At the same time, realize that as you question current practices and consider possible changes, not everyone will agree with you—or be happy with you. If you're a leader, people may leave your church. If you're submitted to the leadership of others, you may be asked to leave. Or you may need to make the choice to connect with another church. In all of these scenarios, remember to love, forgive, and bless those with whom you've had the privilege of sharing life.

If you're a leader in your church or ministry, understand that in altering your philosophy and adjusting your theology, you'll also need to spend time processing the changes with your other leaders. If your leadership team doesn't jointly own this transition, division will follow—sooner or later. It's vital that this step doesn't feel rushed, and that leaders don't feel strong-armed.

As you come to consensus regarding building a collaborative leadership culture, there are some practical ways you can reinforce your decision. One is to share the platform at your weekend gatherings. Regularly seeing and hearing from both men and women will communicate cultural change to any congregation. Giving women more leadership opportunities will improve their skills and increase corporate wisdom. Churches who say they include women, yet exclude them from public meetings, send a mixed message. Another positive step is to speak honorably about one another, celebrating the contributions men and women have made in the life of the church. At the same time, refuse gender-biased jokes. They are literally made at someone else's expense, and will cause great loss to the culture of honor in your church. A positive alternative is to highlight male and female heroes, both from the Bible and from your congregation's daily experiences.

Finally, consult books written by a growing company of godly women and men who have searched the scriptures, persevered in prayer, and immersed themselves in this hard-fought battle for restored togetherness. I conclude with a list of some of the books that have had significant impact on my own life and the life of our church family:

>Barton, Ruth Haley, *Equal to the Task: Men and Women in Partnership* (Downers Grove, Ill.: InterVarsity Press, 1998).

>Bristow, John Temple, *What Paul Really Said About Women* (San Francisco, CA: Harper Collins Publishers, 1991).

>Caine, Christine, *Unashamed: Drop the Baggage, Pick Up Your Freedom, Fulfill Your Destiny* (Grand Rapids, MI: Zondervan, 2016).

Cole, Kadi, *Developing Female Leaders: Navigate the Minefields and Release the Potential of Women in Your Church* (Nashville, TN: Thomas Nelson, 2019).

Cunningham, Loren, and Hamilton, David Joel, *Why Not Women?: A Fresh Look at Scripture on Women in Missions, Ministry, and Leadership* (Seattle, WA: Youth With A Mission Publishing, 2000).

Grady, J. Lee, *Fearless Daughters of the Bible: What You Can Learn from 22 Women Who Challenged Tradition, Fought Injustice and Dared to Lead* (Lake Mary, FL: Charisma House, 2012).

Grenz, Stanley J., *Women in the Church: A Biblical Theology of Women in Ministry* (Downers Grove, IL: InterVarsity Press, 1995).

Henderson, Jim, *The Resignation of Eve* (Carol Stream, IL: Tyndale House Publishers, Inc., 2012).

Jacobs, Cindy, *Women, Rise Up!* (Bloomington, MN: Chosen Books, 2019).

Jones, Beth, *Breaking Through the Stained-Glass Ceiling: Shattering Myths and Empowering Women for Leadership in the Church* (Tulsa, OK: Harrison House Publishers, 2014).

Jordan, Denise, *The Forgotten Feminine* (Taupo, New Zealand: Father Heart Ministries, 2013).

Keener, Craig, *Paul, Women, and Wives: Marriage and Women's Ministry in the Letters of Paul* (Peabody, MA: Hendrickson, 1992).

Kostenberger, Andraeas, and Thomas Schreiner, *Women in the Church: An Analysis and Application of 1 Timothy 2:9-15* (Grand Rapids, MI: Baker Academic, 2016).

Kroeger, Richard Clark and Catherine Clark Kroeger, *I Suffer Not a Woman: Rethinking 1 Timothy 2:11-15 in Light of Ancient Evidence* (Grand Rapids, MI: Baker Books, 2003).

Olson, Phill, *The Other Half of the Army: Women in Kingdom Ministry* (Mechanicsburg, PA: Global Awakening, 2017).

Parish, Fawn, *The Power of Honor* (Camarillo, CA: Conversations, 1999).

Silk, Danny, *Powerful and Free: Confronting the Glass Ceiling for Women in the Church* (Redding, CA: Red Arrow Media, 2015).

Vallotton, Kris, *Fashioned to Reign: Empowering Women to Fulfill Their Divine Destiny* (Minneapolis, MN: Chosen Books, 2013).

I bless you as you continue to write your story. Always remember: wherever Jesus leads us, His love wins and His truth prevails!

"The path of those who do right is like the sun in the morning. It shines brighter and brighter until the full light of day." Proverbs 4:18 (NIRV)

CHAPTER 14

FINAL WORDS

"We need women to rise up as matriarchs alongside our patriarchs in every realm of society so that God's full intention for the planet can be fulfilled."
—Kris Vallotton

When Jesus cried out, "It is finished," His atoning work was completed. Everything necessary for people to be reconciled to God was fully accomplished that day. However, when Jesus said, "I will build My church,"[1] His work was just beginning. The atonement is a finished work. The church is a work in progress.

Building sites can be messy. Being "fitted and held together"[2] sounds poetic, but it can also be painful. Correction is given, sacrifices are made, and adjustments are conceded as our connections are strengthened. Our church's journey was messy. I don't pretend to have done everything right, nor is my presentation airtight. I simply want to share insights we've gleaned in our pursuit of becoming more like Jesus. Yes, I've grown increasingly passionate and confident about my convictions concerning women and men leading together.

Yet I desire to remain always open to discussion, seeking to be "quick to listen and slow to speak."[3]

Like David, I encourage you to be women and men who are "after God's own heart."[4] As you seek Him, you'll find Him to be patient, kind, courageous, and honest. So instead of ending the discussion, I want to start the discussion—many discussions, in fact. We must model a more mature, Christ-like way of dialoguing about our differences.

This issue will not go away. Ignoring it or deploring it won't bring resolve, but rather further hurt and division. In the days prior to the Pentecost outpouring, 120 people gathered in an upper room. Jesus' followers were quite a divergent bunch. A political zealot and a Roman employee? The 'Sons of Thunder"[5] and Barnabas, "the son of consolation"[6]? Peter and the other ten disciples whom he had accused of cowardice? Men and women?

Somehow, they came into "one accord."[7] The root meaning of "accord" is "the harmony of minds, the consent of opinions or wills."[8] Harmony is not unison. It doesn't involve everyone making the same sound. Nor does it include identical belief systems. The body of Christ may never completely agree on every aspect of women and men ministering together. Yet out of our love for Jesus, and for the sake of His Gospel, can we find a way to harmonize our hearts and our opinions?

The collaborative leadership of women and men in the church is an answer to Jesus' petition, "I pray that they all will be one."[9] Our unity is more than equality. It's equity in diversity. Men and women will never be the same, in terms of being identical. But we're part of the same spiritual family. We can love one another with the same love, in the same army, in the same battle, against the same enemy, whom we will overcome with the same power that raised Jesus from the dead!

And we can do this—together!

ENDNOTES

CHAPTER 1
In the Beginning

1. Danny Silk, *Powerful and Free: Confronting the Glass Ceiling for Women in the Church* (Redding, CA: Red Arrow Media, 2015), 67.

2. Everett Ferguson, *Women in the Church: Biblical and Historical Perspectives* (Abilene, TX: Desert Willow Publishing, 2015), 104.

3. Fawn Parish, *The Power of Honor* (Camarillo, CA: Conversations, 1999), 127.

4. Acts 20:27 ESV

5. Matthew 19:24 ESV

6. Parish, *The Power of Honor*, 131.

7. D. J. Wiseman, *The Tyndale Old Testament Commentary: Genesis* (Downers Grove, IL: InterVarsity Press, 1967), 50.

8. Ephesians 2:10 NLT

9. John Barton, and John Muddiman, *The Oxford Bible Commentary* (New York, NY: Oxford University Press, Inc., 2001), 43.

10. George Arthur Buttrick, *The Interpreter's Bible, Volume I: General and Old Testament Articles, Genesis, and Exodus* (New York, NY: Abingdon Press, 1952), 483.

11. Ajith Fernando, *ESV Global Bible* (Wheaton, IL: Crossway Bibles, 2012), 46.

12. Genesis 1:2 ESV

13. John 1:2-3 KJV

14. C. F. Keil, and F. Delitzsch, *Commentary on the Old Testament, Volume I* (Grand Rapids, MI: William B. Eerdmans Publishing Company, 1980), 62.

15. Frank E. Gaebelein, *The Expositor's Bible Commentary-Volume 2* (Grand Rapids, MI: Zondervan Publishing House, 1990), 37.

16. Ferguson, *Women in the Church*, 102.

17. Genesis 1:27 KJV

18. Raymond C. Ortlund Jr., *Male-Female Equality and Male Headship: Genesis 1-3*, Bible.org. April 11, 2005, Accessed September 20, 2016, 1-3.

19. Genesis 2:20

20. Thomas R. Schreiner, *Women in the Church: An Interpretation and Application of 1 Timothy 2:9-15* (Wheaton, IL: Crossway, 2016), 206.

21. J.A. Emerton, *Studies in the Pentateuch* (Leiden, Netherlands: Brill, 1991), 15.

22. Fernando, *ESV Global Bible*, 47.

23. Psalm 103:13 KJV

24. Isaiah 66:13 KJV

25. John 4:24 NIV

26. Miguel A. De La Torre, *Belief: A Theological Commentary on the Bible-Genesis* (Louisville, KY: Westminster John Knox Press, 2011), 23.

27. De La Torre, *Belief*, 246.

28. Charles M. Laymon, *The Interpreter's One-Volume Commentary on the Bible* (Nashville, TN: Abingdon Press, 1971), 4.

29. Bruce M. Metzger, *The Oxford Companion to the Bible* (New York, NY: Oxford University Press, 1993), 806.

30. Genesis 2:18 KJV

31. Genesis 2:21-22 KJV

32. Genesis 2:24 KJV

33. Exodus 18:4; Deuteronomy 33:26; Psalm 33:20; 70:6; 115:9; 121:1

34. Mignon R. Jacobs, *Gender, Power, and Persuasion: The Genesis Narratives and Contemporary Portraits* (Grand Rapids, MI: Baker Academic, 2007), 41.

35. John 5:30 NIV

36. John 4:14 NIV

37. Jacobs, *Gender, Power, and Persuasion*, 41.

38. Phyllis Trible, *God and the Rhetoric of Sexuality* (Philadelphia, PA: Fortress Press, 1978), 90.

39. Wiseman, *The Tyndale Old Testament Commentary*, 52.

40. Ronald W. Pierce and Rebecca Merrill Groothius, *Discovering Biblical Equality: Complementarity Without Hierarchy* (Downer's Grove, IL: IVP Academic, 2005), 87.

41. *A Concise Hebrew and Aramaic Lexicon of the Old Testament* (Grand Rapids, MI: William B Eerdmans Publishing Company, 1972), 5.

42. Pierce, *Discovering Biblical Equality*, 87.

43. Keil, *Commentary on the Old Testament, Volume I*, 65.

44. Beverly Stratton, *Out of Eden: Reading Rhetoric, and Ideology in Genesis 2-3,* Journal for the Study of the Old Testament: Supplement Series 208. (Sheffield, UK: Sheffield Academic Press, 1995), 37.

45. Rebecca Merrill Groothius, *Good News for Women: A Biblical Picture of Gender Equality* (Grand Rapids, MI: Baker Books, 1996), 137.

46. Genesis 2:23 KJV

47. George. W. Ramsey, "Is Name-Giving an Act of Domination in Genesis 2:23 and Elsewhere?" *The Catholic Biblical Quarterly* Vol. 50, No. 1, 50th Anniversary Volume (January, 1988): 35, https://www.jstor.org/stable/43717586?seq=1.

48. Jacobs, *Gender, Power, and Persuasion*, 28.

49. Genesis 2:23 ESV

50. Schreiner, *Women in the Church*, 206.

51. Pierce, *Discovering Biblical Equality*, 87.

52. *A Concise Hebrew and Aramaic Lexicon of the Old Testament*, 7.

53. Genesis 1:28 KJV

54. Wiseman, *The Tyndale Old Testament Commentary*, 52.

55. Genesis 1:26 NIV

56. Genesis 2:18 NIV

CHAPTER 2
Disharmony, Disunity, and the Fall of Humanity

1. Ephesians 1:4-5 MSG

2. Genesis 1:31 KJV

3. Genesis 3:1 NIV

4. Barton, *the Oxford Bible Commentary*, 44.

5. Genesis 3:1 KJV

6. Jacobs, *Gender, Power, and Persuasion*, 47.

7. H. Orton Wiley, *Christian Theology, Volume II* (Kansas City, MO: Beacon Hill Press, 1952), 35.

8. 2 Corinthians 11:3 KJV

9. Genesis 3:1 NIV

10. Wiseman, *The Tyndale Old Testament Commentary*, 67.

11. Wiseman, *The Tyndale Old Testament Commentary*, 68.

12. Ephraim A. Speiser, *The Anchor Bible: Genesis* (Garden City, NY: Doubleday & Company, Inc., 1964), 23.

13. Pierce, *Discovering Biblical Authority*, 89.

14. Genesis 3:3 NIV

15. Loren Cunningham, and David Joel Hamilton, *Why Not Women?: A Fresh Look at Scripture on Women in Missions, Ministry, and Leadership* (Seattle, WA: Youth With A Mission Publishing, 2000), 223.

16. Genesis 3:2 NIV

17. Ferguson, *Women in the Church*, 103.

18. Genesis 3:6 NRSV

19. Jacobs, *Gender, Power, and Persuasion*, 59.

20. Genesis 3:6 NIV

21. Pierce, *Discovering Biblical Equality*, 89.

22. Jacobs, *Gender, Power, and Persuasion*, 42.

23. Jan P. Fokkleman, *Narrative Art in Genesis: Specimens of Stylistic and Structural Analysis* (Eugene, OR: Wipf & Stock, Publishers, 2004), 47.

24. Fokkleman, *Narrative Art in Genesis*, 47.

25. Fokkleman, *Narrative Art in Genesis*, 48.

26. Pierce, *Discovering Biblical Equality*, 90.

27. Wiley, *Christian Theology, Volume II*, 37.

28. Genesis 2:25 KJV

29. Wiseman, *The Tyndale Old Testament Commentary*, 69.

30. Alfred Edersheim, *Bible History of the Old Testament* (Grand Rapids, MI: William B. Eerdman's Publishing Company, 1982), 21.

31. Carol Meyers, *Discovering Eve: Ancient Israelite Women in Context* (New York, NY: Oxford University Press, USA, 1991), 27.

32. Laymon, *The Interpreter's One-Volume Commentary of the Bible*, 6.

33. Pierce, *Discovering Biblical Equality*, 91.

34. Keil, *Commentary on the Old Testament, Volume I*, 103.

35. Genesis 3:16b NIV

36. Meyers, *Discovering Eve: Ancient Israelite Women in Context*, 28.

37. Keil, *Commentary on the Old Testament, Volume I*, 103.

38. Meyers, *Discovering Eve*, 28.

39. Keil, *Commentary on the Old Testament, Volume I*, 103.

40. Buttrick, *The Interpreter's Bible, Volume I*, 510.

41. Jacobs, *Gender, Power, and Persuasion*, 68.

42. Genesis 3:16 KJV

43. Genesis 3:17 KJV

44. De La Torre, *Belief*, 86.

45. De La Torre, *Belief*, 87.

46. Fernando, *ESV Global Bible*, 63.

47. Fernando, *ESV Global Bible*, 64.

48. Keil, *Commentary on the Old Testament, Volume I*, 103.

49. Matthew 18:11 NASB

CHAPTER 3
Old Testament Glimpses of the Restoration of God's Original Intent

1. Ruth Haley Barton, *How I Changed My Mind About Women in Leadership* (Grand Rapids, MI: Zondervan, 2011), 43.

2. Genesis 16 NKJV

3. Genesis 19:1-8

4. Barton, *How I Changed My Mind About Women in Leadership*, 43.

5. Exodus 15:20 NIV

6. Micah 6:4 NIV

7. 2 Kings 22 NIV

8. Isaiah 8:3 NKJV

9. Judges 4:4,6-7 NIV

10. Judges 4:5 NIV

11. Judges 5:7 NIV

12. Judges 4:5; Deuteronomy 17:8 NIV

13. Judges 4:5 NIV

14. Pierce, *Discovering Biblical Equality*, 113.

15. Pierce, *Discovering Biblical Equality*, 113.

16. Judges 4:6-7 NIV

17. Judges 4:8 NIV

18. Judges 4:18 NIV

19. Judges 5:2 NIV

20. Nahum 3:8; Habakkuk 1:6; Jeremiah 1:2; Zephaniah 1:1 NKJV

21. 2 Kings 22:13-14 NIV

22. Phyllis Bird, "*The Place of Women in the Israelite Cultus,*" in *Ancient Israelite Religion*. (Philadelphia, PA: Fortress, 1987), 397.

23. Exodus 35:22-26

24. Exodus 38:8; 1 Samuel 2:22

25. Psalm 68:25; Judges 21:19-23

26. 1 Samuel 18:7; 2 Chronicles 35:25; Ezra 2:65; Nehemiah 7:67; 1 Samuel 1:24-25

27. Andreas Kostenberger and Margaret Kostenberger, *God's Design for Man and Woman: A Biblical Theological Survey* (Wheaton, IL: Crossway, 2014), 72.

28. Joel 2:29 NIV

CHAPTER 4
The High Cost of Compromise

1. Herbert Danby, *Tractate Sanhedrin, Mishnah and Tosefta: The Judicial Procedure of the Jews* (London: Forgotten Books, 2008), 48.

2. Mark Cartwright, "The Role of Women in the Roman World" in *Ancient History Encyclopedia* Ancient History Encyclopedia, 22 February, 2014, accessed 15 August, 2019, https://www.ancient.eu/article/659/the-role-of-women-in-the-roman-world/.

3. *Babylonian Talmud: Tractate Baba Bathra*, Folio 58a.

4. Cunningham, *Why Not Women?*, 16.

5. Cunningham, Why Not Women?, 18.

6. Judith Romney Wegner, *Chattel or Person? The Status of Women in the Mishnah* (London: Oxford University Press, 1992), 42.

7. Wegner, *Chattel or Person?*, 48.

8. Michael Lustig, *Herod's Temple* (CreateSpace Independent Publishing Platform, 2017), 53.

9. *Yerushalmi, Sotah* 3:4.

10. *Talmud, Berachot* 43b.

CHAPTER 5
Jesus the Revolutionary Restorer

1. John 10:23

2. Alvera Mickelson, *Women, Authority, and the Bible* (Downer's Grove, IL: InterVarsity Press, 1986), 70.

3. Luke 10:38-42

4. Acts 22:3

5. Luke 8:1-3

6. Matthew 6:5

7. Luke 8:43; 13:16

8. Matthew 28:9-10

CHAPTER 6
Pioneering Partnerships

1. Acts 1:22

2. Luke 23:49, 55

3. Luke 24:10

4. Matthew 27:56

5. Mark 15:40,41; John 19:25

6. Mark 14:43-52

7. Matthew 26:33

8. Luke 22:54-62

9. John 19:25

10. Luke 24:11

11. Acts 2:1

12. Acts 2:41

13. Acts 2:34-47

14. Acts 8:3 NASB

15. Acts 22:4-5

16. John Temple Bristow, *What Paul Really Said About Women* (San Francisco: Harper Collins, 1991), 55.

17. Acts 16:11-15

18. Acts 16:14

19. Acts 17:4, 11-12

20. Acts 17:34

21. Philippians 4:2-3 NIV

22. 1 Corinthians 16:19

23. Acts 18:2-3, 18-28

24. Romans 16:3 NIV

25. Romans 17:4 NIV

26. Romans 16:1

27. Romans 16:2

28. 1 Corinthians 3:4

29. Romans 16:7 NIV

30. Eddie Hyatt, *Paul, Women, and the Church* (Grapevine, TX: Hyatt International Ministries, Incorporated, 2016), 25.

31. F.F. Bruce, *Paul: Apostle of the Heart Set Free* (Grand Rapids, MI: Eerdmans, 1977), 15.

32. 1 Corinthians 1:11

33. Colossians 4:15

34. 2 Timothy 2:2 TPT

35. Cunningham *Why Not Women?*, 221.

36. Acts 2:17-18; 21:8-9; 18:26; 2 Timothy 1:5; Titus 2:2-5

37. 1 Timothy 5:1-2

38. Titus 2:3-5

39. Colossians 4:15; 1 Corinthians 1:11; 16:19

40. 2 John 1:1 NIV

CHAPTER 7
Declaration of Interdependence

1. Galatians 5:6

2. Galatians 5:15 TPT

3. Philippians 3:5

4. Romans 7:19-24

5. Galatians 3:24

6. Joseph Thayer, *Thayer's Greek Definitions* (Boston, MA: Hendrickson Publishers, 1996), 426.

7. Gerhard Friedrich, *Theological Dictionary of the New Testament* (Grand Rapids, MI: William B. Eerdmans Publishing Company, 1967), 620.

8. Lee Haines, Armor D. Peisker and Howard A. Hanke, *The Wesleyan Bible Commentary, Volume One, Part1: Genesis and Exodus* (Grand Rapids, MI: William B. Eerdmans Publishing Company, 1967), 620.

9. Laymon, *The Interpreter's One-Volume Commentary on the Bible*, 831.

10. Laymon, *The Interpreter's One-Volume Commentary on the Bible*, 832.

11. Barton, *The Oxford Bible Commentary*, 1160.

12. Wilber T. Dayton, *The Wesleyan Bible Commentary, Volume Five, Part I: Romans and Galatians* (Grand Rapids, MI: William B. Eerdmans Publishing Company, 1965), 349.

13. Dayton, *The Wesleyan Bible Commentary, Volume Five, Part I: Romans and Galatians*, 350.

14. Genesis 1:26 KJV

15. Galatians 3:26 NIV

16. Galatians 3:26 KJV

17. F.F. Bruce, *The New International Greek Testament Commentary: The Epistle to the Galatians- A Commentary on the Greek Text* (Grand Rapids, MI: William B. Eerdmans Publishing Company, 1982), 183.

18. Bruce, *The New International Greek Testament Commentary*, 185.

19. Galatians 6:15 TPT

20. Galatians 3:27 NIV

21. David H. Stern, *Jewish New Testament Commentary* (Clarksville, MD: Jewish New Testament Publications, Inc., 1996), 553.

22. Bruce, *The New International Greek Testament Commentary*, 184.

23. Henry Alford, *Alford's Greek Testament: An Exegetical and Critical Commentary- Volume III Galatians-Philemon* (Grand Rapids, MI: Guardian Press, 1856), 38.

24. Galatians 3:27 NIV

25. Bruce, *The New International Greek Testament Commentary*, 186.

26. J. Louis Martyn, *The Anchor Yale Bible: Galatians* (London, UK: Yale University Press, 1997), 374.

27. Bruce, *The New International Greek Testament Commentary*, 190.

28. Galatians 3:28 NIV

29. Barton, *The Oxford Bible Commentary*, 1163.

30. Archibald Thomas Robertson, *Word Pictures in the New Testament* (Nashville, TN: Broadman Press, 1931), 299.

31. Buttrick, *The Interpreter's Bible*, 519.

32. Buttrick, *The Interpreter's Bible*, 519.

33. Josephus, *Against Apion II*, 24.

34. Stern, *Jewish New Testament Commentary*, 555.

35. J.H. Hertz, *The Authorized Daily Prayer Book* (New York, NY: Bloch Publishing Company, revised edition, 1948), 28.

36. Bruce, *The New International Greek Testament Commentary*, 190.

37. Dayton, *The Wesleyan Bible Commentary, Volume Five, Part I: Romans and Galatians*, 349.

38. William Barclay, *The Letters to the Galatians and Ephesians* (Philadelphia, PA: The Westminster Press, 1976), 33.

39. Bruce, *The New International Greek Testament Commentary*, 187.

40. Henry Alford, *Alford's Greek Testament*, 37.

41. Genesis 3:16

42. Herman Ridderbos, *The New International Commentary on the New Testament: The Epistle of Paul to the Churches of Galatia* (Grand Rapids, MI: William B. Eerdmans Publishing, 1953), 149.

43. Pierce, *Discovering Biblical Equality*, 181.

44. Ferguson, *Women in the Church*, 108.

45. Ferguson, *Women in the Church*, 109.

46. Ferguson, *Women in the Church*, 108.

47. Bruce, *The New International Greek Testament Commentary*, 190.

48. Romans 12:5 KJV

49. Bruce, *The New International Greek Testament Commentary*, 190.

50. Buttrick, *The Interpreter's Bible*, 520.

51. Buttrick, *The Interpreter's Bible*, 520.

52. 1 Corinthians 11:10

53. Romans 16:3-4

54. Acts 18:26

55. 2 Timothy 1:5

56. Bruce, *The New International Greek Testament Commentary*, 190.

57. Pierce, *Discovering Biblical Equality*, 185.

58. Parish, *The Power of Honor*, 126.

CHAPTER 8
1 Timothy 2:11-15 in Context

1. Mickelsen, *Women, Authority, and the Bible*, 95.

2. Stanley N. Gundry and James R. Beck, *Two Views on Women in Ministry* (Grand Rapids, MI: Zondervan, 2005), 21.

3. Gundry, *Two Views on Women in Ministry*, 23.

4. Denise Jordan, *The Forgotten Feminine* (Taupo, New Zealand: Father Heart Ministries, 2013), 33.

5. Wayne Grudum, *Biblical Foundations for Manhood and Womanhood* (Wheaton, IL: Crossway, 2002), 147.

6. Genesis 2:18 NIV

7. Carolyn Custis James, *Half the Church: Recapturing God's Global Vision for Women* (Grand Rapids, MI: Zondervan, 2011), 112.

8. Proverbs 31:27 NIV

9. Proverbs 31:23, NIV

10. Stanley J. Grenz, *Women in the Church: A Biblical Theology of Women in Ministry* (Downers Grove: InterVarsity Press, 1995), 66.

11. Pamela J. Scalise, "Women in Ministry: Reclaiming Our Old Testament Heritage," *Review and Expositor* 83, no. 1 (Winter 1986), 8.

12. Grenz, *Women in the Church*, 67.

13. Gundry, *Two Views of Women in Ministry*, 36.

14. Romans 16:7

15. Acts 21:9; 1 Corinthians 11:5

16. Philippians 4:2-3

17. Acts 12:12; 16:14-15; Colossians 4:15

18. Pierce, *Discovering Biblical Equality*, 241.

19. Alvin John Schmidt, *Veiled and Silenced: How Culture Shaped Sexist Theology* (Macon, GA: Mercer University Press, 1989), 149.

20. Johannes Quasten, *Ancient Christian Writers* (London, UK: Longmans, 1960), 414.

21. Grenz, *Women in the Church*, 43.

22. Ruth Tucker and Walter Liefield, *Daughters of the Church: Women and Ministry from New Testament Times to the Present* (Grand Rapids, MI: Zondervan, 1987), 252.

23. Tucker, *Daughters of the Church*, 253.

24. Pierce, *Discovering Biblical Equality*, 205.

25. 1 Timothy 1:3 NIV

26. E. Randolph Richards and Brandon J. O'Brian, *Misreading Scriptures with Western Eyes* (Downers Grove, IL: IVP Books, 2012), 169-170.

27. 1 Timothy 6:20-21 NIV

28. 2 Timothy 3:1-9 NIV

29. Pierce, *Discovering Biblical Equality*, 219.

30. 1 Timothy 2:15 RSV

31. Pierce, *Discovering Biblical Equality*, 219

32. 1 Timothy 3:1-13

33. 1 Timothy 5:20

34. 1 Timothy 6:4-5

35. 1 Timothy 5:15; 6:20-21 NIV

36. 1 Timothy 2:12

37. 1 Timothy 2:8

38. Mary J. Evans, *Women in the Bible* (Downers Grove, IL: InterVarsity Press, 1983), 107.

39. James N. Watkins, "A Case for Women in Ministry," *Hope and Humor*, 2009, https://www.jameswatkins.com/articles-2/heavy/women/.

40. 1 Timothy 2:12 RSV, NAB, TEV, NASB, NKJV, NIV, NLT, ESV.

41. Richard Clark Kroeger and Catherine Clark Kroeger, *I Suffer Not a Woman: Rethinking 1 Timothy 2:11-15 in Light of Ancient Evidence* (Grand Rapids, MI: Baker Books, 2003), 83.

42. Kroeger, *I Suffer Not a Woman*, 84.

43. Kroeger, *I Suffer Not a Woman*, 84.

44. Pierce, *Discovering Biblical Equality*, 263.

45. E. Randolph Richards and Brandon J. O'Brien, *Misreading Scriptures with Western Eyes* (Downers Grove, IL: IVP Books, 2012), 169-170.

46. 2 Timothy 1:5

47. Colossians 3:16

48. 1 Corinthians 14:26

49. 1 Corinthians 14:31

50. John Piper and Wayne Grudum, *Recovering Biblical Manhood and Womanhood: A Response*

to Evangelical Feminism (Wheaton, IL: Crossway, 2006), 69.

51. Piper, *Recovering Biblical Manhood and Womanhood*, 70.

52. Kris Vallotton, *Fashioned to Reign: Empowering Women to Fulfill Their Divine Destiny* (Minneapolis, MN: Chosen Books, 2013), 177.

53. Pierce, *Discovering Biblical Equality*, 211.

54. Josephus, *Jewish Wars I* (Cambridge, MA: Harvard University Press, 1927), 582.

55. Kroeger, *I Suffer Not a Woman*, 84.

56. Kroeger, *I Suffer Not a Woman*, 91.

57. Kostenberger, *Women in the Church*, 51.

58. Mickelsen, *Women, Authority, and the Bible*, 296.

59. C.S. Lewis, "Priestesses in the Church?" in *God in the Dock*, ed. Walter Hooper (Grand Rapids, MI: Eerdmans, 1994), 236.

60. Gundry, *Two Views on Women in Ministry*, 169.

61. Piper, *Recovering Biblical Manhood and Womanhood*, 60-61.

62. Phoebe Palmer, *Promise of the Father: A Neglected Specialty of the Last Days* (Eugene, OR: Wipf and Stock, 2015), 49-50.

63. Gundry, *Two Views on Women in Ministry*, 248.

64. Bill Gaultiere, "Women as Pastors, Elders, and Leaders in Bible-Based Churches," *Soul Shepherding*, https://www.soulshepherding.org/women-pastors-elders-leaders-bible-based-christian-churches/.

65. Craig Keener, *Paul, Women, and Wives: Marriage and Women's Ministry in the Letters of Paul* (Peabody, MA: 1992), 101.

66. Craig Keener, *Paul, Women, and Wives*, 108-109.

67. Craig Keener, *Paul, Women, and Wives*, 112.

68. Cunningham, *Why Not Women*, 221.

69. 2 Timothy 2:2 KJV

70. 2 Timothy 2:2 NIV

71. Cunningham, *Why Not Women?*, 221

72. Vallotton, *Fashioned to Reign*, 177.

73. Grenz, *Women in the Church*, 174.

74. Christine Caine, *Unashamed: Drop the Baggage, Pick Up Your Freedom, Fulfill Your Destiny* (Grand Rapids, MI: 2018), 77.

75. 1 Timothy 2:11 NIV

76 Gaultiere, "Women as Pastors, Elders, and Leaders in Bible-Based Churches."

77. Rachel Held Evans, *A Year of Biblical Womanhood: How a Liberated Woman Found Herself Sitting on Her Roof, Covering Her Head, and Calling Her Husband "Master"* (Nashville, TN: Thomas Nelson, 2012), 72.

78. Beth Jones, *Breaking Through the Stained Glass Ceiling: Shattering Myths and Empowering Women for Leadership in the Church* (Tulsa, OK: Harrison House Publishers, 2014), 111.

79. Ephesians 5:21-26

80. Cunningham, *Why Not Women?*, 69.

CHAPTER 9
What About Those Other Verses?

1. John Temple Bristow, *What Paul Really Said About Women* (New York, NY: HarperCollins Publishers, 1988), 106.

2. John Temple Bristow, *What Paul Really Said About Women*, 106.

3. 1 Timothy 3:1 ESV

4. Cunningham, *Why Not Women?*, 227.

5. 1 Timothy 3:5

6. *Strong's Exhaustive Concordance of the Bible* (Nashville, TN: Thomas Nelson, 2010), 1380.

7. Cunningham, *Why Not Women?*, 229.

8. Cunningham, *Why Not Women?*, 229.

9. Phil Olson, *The Other Half of the Army: Women in Kingdom Ministry* (Mechanicsburg: PA, Phil Olson), 68.

10. 1 Timothy 3:11 NIV, NASB, ERV, YLT

11. 1 Timothy 2:11-15

12. Cunningham, *Why Not Women?*, 230.

13. Hyatt, *Paul, Women, and the Church*, 46.

14. Hyatt, *Paul, Women, and the Church*, 46.

15. Ephesians 4:11-12 KJV

16. Grenz, *Women in the Church*, 215.

17. Luke 14:7,8

18. 1 Timothy 3:1 NIV

19. Grenz, *Women in the Church*, 215.

20. 1 Corinthians 11:11 NIV

21. 1 Corinthians 14:1

22. 1 Corinthians 14:5 NIV

23. 1 Corinthians 14:31 NIV

24. 1 Corinthians 11:4-5

25. Gene Edwards, *The Christian Woman Set Free: Women Freed from Second-Class Citizenship in the Kingdom of God* (Jacksonville, FL: Seedsowers Publishing House, 2005), 101.

26. 1 Corinthians 11:17-22

27. Cunningham, *Why Not Women?*, 187.

28. 1 Corinthians 14:26-28

29. 1 Corinthians 14:29-33

30. 1 Corinthians 14:34-35

31. 1 Corinthians 14:28

32. 1 Corinthians 14:30

33. 1 Corinthians 14:34

34. 1 Corinthians 14:31

35. 1 Corinthians 14:32

36. 1 Corinthians 14:31 NIV

37. 1 Corinthians 14:35

38. Cunningham, *Why Not Women?*, 201.

39. 1 Corinthians 11:7-10

40. *Strong's Exhaustive Concordance of the Bible*, 1520.

41. Titus Maccius Plautus, *Little Carthaginian*, Quoted in F.H. Sandbach, *The Comic Theatre of Greece and Rome* (New York, NY: Norton, 1977), 109.

42. Mishnah Gittin, 4.8.

43. 1 Corinthians 7:1

44. 1 Corinthians 14:36 KJV

45. 1 Corinthians 14:36 NIV

46. 1 Corinthians 14:40 NIV

47. 1 Corinthians 14:33 NIV

CHAPTER 10
A Tale of Two Women

1. Patricia Hill, *The World Their Household: The American Woman's Foreign Missions Movement and Cultural Transformation, 1870-1920* (Ann Arbor, MI: University of Michigan, 1985), 2.

2. Pierce, *Discovering Biblical Equality*, 23.

3. Pierce, *Discovering Biblical Equality*, 24.

4. Samuel DeWitt Proctor, *The Substance of Things Hoped For: A Memoir of the African-American Faith* (Valley Forge, PA: Judson Press, 1999), 233.

5. Danny Silk, *Powerful and Free: Confronting the Glass Ceiling for Women in the Church* (Redding, CA: Red Arrow Media, 2015), 48.

6. Paul L. King, *Anointed Women: The Rich Heritage of Women in Ministry in the Christian and Missionary Alliance* (Tulsa, OK: Word & Spirit Press, 2009), 19.

7. Johnny Enlow, *The Seven Mountain Renaissance* (New Kensington, PA: Whitaker House, 2015), 45.

8. Eleanor McLaughlin, *Women of Spirit: Female Leaders in the Jewish and Christian Traditions* (New York, NY: Simon & Shuster, 1979), 143.

9. Enlow, *The Seven Mountain Renaissance*, 43.

10. McLaughlin, *Women of Spirit*, 153.

11. Enlow, *The Seven Mountain Renaissance*, 47.

12. Susan Hill Lindley, *"You Have Stept Out of Your Place": A History of Women and Religion in America* (Louisville, KY: Westminster John Knox Press, 1996), 10.

13. Francis J. Bremer, *Anne Hutchinson: Troubler of the Puritan Zion* (Huntington, NY: Robert E. Krieger Publishing Company, 1981), 1.

14. Bremer, *Anne Hutchinson*, 2.

15. Priscilla Pope-Levison, *Building the Old-Time Religion: Women Evangelists in the Progressive Era* (New York, NY: New York University Press, 2014), 37.

16. Lindley, *"You Have Stept Out of Your Place"*, 2.

17. Lindley, *"You Have Stept Out of Your Place"*, 2.

18. Bremer, *Anne Hutchinson*, 3.

19. Pope-Levison, *Building the Old-Time Religion*, 42.

20. Bremer, *Anne Hutchinson*, 4.

21. Bremer, *Anne Hutchinson*, 4.

22. Bremer, *Anne Hutchinson*, 4.

23. Pierce, *Discovering Biblical Equality*, 39.

24. Bremer, *Anne Hutchinson*, 5.

25. John Cotton, *The Antinomian Controversy* (Middletown, CT: Wesleyan University Press, 1968), 412.

26. Bremer, *Anne Hutchinson*, 4.

27. Cotton, *The Antinomian Controversy*, 415.

28. Bremer, *Anne Hutchinson*, 4.

29. Lindley, *"You Have Stept Out of Your Place"*, 2.

30. Mary Maples Dunn, *Saints and Sisters: Congregational and Quaker Women in the Early Colonial*

Period (American Quarterly, Vol. 30, No. 5, "Special Issue: Women and Religion" (Winter, 1978), 595.

31. Dunn, *Saints and Sisters*, 596.

32. Lyle Koehler, *The Case of the American Jezebels: Anne Hutchinson and female agitation during the years of the Antinomian turmoil, 1636-1640* (New York, NY: William and Mary Quarterly, 31, 1974), 58.

33. Koehler, *The Case of the American Jezebels*, 59.

34. Koehler, *The Case of the American Jezebels*, 59.

35. Koehler, *The Case of the American Jezebels*, 59.

36. Ben Barker-Benfield, *"Anne Hutchinson and the Puritan Attitude Toward Women,"* Feminist Studies, Vol. 1, No. 2 (Autumn 1972), published by Feminist Studies, Inc., : 76, https://www.jstor.org/stable/3177641?read-now=1&seq=1#page_scan_tab_contents.

37. Barker-Benfield, *"Anne Hutchinson and the Puritan Attitude Toward Women,"* 73.

38. Selma Williams, *Divine Rebel: The Life of Anne Marbury Hutchinson* (New York, NY: Holt, Rinehart, and Winston, 1981), 121.

39. Williams, *Divine Rebel*, 121.

40. Ann Braude, *Sisters and Saints: Women and American Religion* (New York, NY: Oxford University Press, 2001), 32.

41. Ann Braude, *Sisters and Saints*, 32.

42. Ann Braude, *Sisters and Saints*, 32.

43. Lindley, *"You Have Stept Out of Your Place"*, 2.

44. John Winthrop, *Winthrop's Journal: History of New England, 1630-1649* (New York, NY: Scribner, 1908), 213.

45. Lindley, *"You Have Stept Out of Your Place"*, 3.

46. Lindley, *"You Have Stept Out of Your Place"*, 3.

47. Thomas Weld, *The Antinomian Controversy: 1636-1638: A Documentary History* (Middletown, CT: Wesleyan University Press, 1968), 382.

48. Bremer, *Anne Hutchinson: Troubler of the Puritan Zion*, 4.

49. Bremer, *Anne Hutchinson: Troubler of the Puritan Zion*, 4.

50. Weld, *The Antinomian Controversy*, 387

51. Bremer, *Anne Hutchinson*, 5.

52. Bremer, *Anne Hutchinson*, 6.

53. Winthrop, *Winthrop's Journal*, 240.

54. Lindley, *"You Have Stept Out of Your Place"*, 4.

55. Lindley, *"You Have Stept Out of Your Place"*, 4.

56. Richard B. Morris, *"Jezebel Before the Judges"* (New York, NY: Harpers, 1967).

57. Bremer, *Anne Hutchinson*, 6.

58. Bremer, *Anne Hutchinson*, 6.

59. Weld, *The Antinomian Controversy*, 342.

60. Bremer, *Anne Hutchinson*, 6.

61. Williams, *Divine Rebel*, 278.

62. Weld, *The Antinomian Controversy*, 6.

63. Braude, *Sisters and Saints*, 35.

64. Richard S. Newman, *Freedom's Prophet: Bishop Richard Alan* (New York, NY: NYU Press, 2008), 220.

65. Susan Ditmire, *"Mrs. Jarena Lee, First Black Woman Preacher in the A.M.E. Church, 1820, Daughter of Cape May County,"* UsGenNet, Posted- September 2, 2012, http://www.usgennet.org/usa/nj/county/capemay/Jarena.htm.

66. Elizabeth Elkin Grammar, *Some Wild Visions: Autobiographies by Female Itinerant Evangelists in 19th Century America* (New York, NY: Oxford University Press, 1986), 2.

67. Ditmire, *"Mrs. Jarena Lee, First Black Woman Preacher in the A.M.E."*

68. William I. Andrews, *Sisters of the Spirit: Three Black Women's Autobiographies of the Nineteenth Century* (Bloomington, IN: Indiana University Press, 1986), 2.

69. Ditmire, *"Mrs. Jarena Lee, First Black Woman Preacher in the A.M.E."*

70. Newman, *Freedom's Prophet*, 215.

71. Jarena Lee, *Religious Experience and Journal of Mrs. Jarena Lee: Giving an Account of Her Call to Preach the Gospel* (Philadelphia, PA: By the Author, 1849), 141.

72. Ditmire, *"Mrs. Jarena Lee, First Black Woman Preacher in the A.M.E."*

73. Braude, *Sisters and Saints*, 30.

74. Elizabeth J. Clapp, *Mothers of All Children: Women Reformers and the Rise of Juvenile Courts in Progressive-Era America* (University Park, PA: Pennsylvania State University Press, 1998), 3.

75. Braude, *Sisters and Saints*, 30.

76. Lee, *Religious Experience and Journal of Mrs. Jarena Lee*, 141.

77. Susie C. Stanley, *Holy Boldness: Women Preachers' Autobiographies and the Sanctified Self* (Knoxville, TN: The University of Tennessee Press, 2002), 12.

78. Lee, *Religious Experience and Journal of Mrs. Jarena Lee*, 141.

79. Andrews, *Sisters of the Spirit*, 14.

80. Liz Stanley, *The Autobiographical I* (Manchester, IN: Manchester University Press, 1992), 114.

81. Stanley, *Holy Boldness*, 99.

82. Stanley, *Holy Boldness*, 100.

83. Stanley, *The Autobiographical I*, 121.

84. Stanley, *Holy Boldness*, 190.

85. Ditmire, "*Mrs. Jarena Lee, First Black Woman Preacher in the A.M.E.*"

86. Stanley, *Holy Boldness*, 207.

87. Andrews, *Sisters of the Spirit*, 3.

88. Lee, *Religious Experience and Journal of Mrs. Jarena Lee*, 21.

89. Andrews, *Sisters of the Spirit*, 11.

90. Elaw Lee, *At Odds: Women and the Family in America* (New York, NY: Oxford Press, 1980), 210.

91. Andrews, *Sisters of the Spirit*, 21.

92. Ditmire, "*Mrs. Jarena Lee, First Black Woman Preacher in the A.M.E.*"

93. Andrews, *Sisters of the Spirit*, 210.

94. Ditmire, *"Mrs. Jarena Lee, First Black Woman Preacher in the A.M.E."*

95. Pierce, *Discovering Biblical Equality*, 37.

96. Estrelda Alexander and Amos Yong, *Philip's Daughters: Women in Pentecostal-Charismatic Leadership* (Eugene, OR: Pickwick Publications, 2009), 136.

97. Alexander, *Philip's Daughters*, 133.

98. Palmer, *Promise of the Father*, 34.

99. Alexander, *Philip's Daughters*, 147.

100. Susan C. Hyatt, *In the Spirit We're Equal: The Spirit, the Bible, and Women- A Revival Perspective* (Tulsa, OK: Hyatt Press, 1998), 42-43.

101. Keener, *Paul, Women, and Wives*, 121.

CHAPTER 11
Their Stories

1. Ephesians 4:16 TPT

2. Beth Moore, "A Letter to My Brothers," from *The LPM Blog (blog.lproof.org)*. All rights reserved. Used by permission.

3. Eileen Vincent, *God Can Do It Here* (London, England: Marshall, M & S, 1982).

CHAPTER 12
Our Story

1. 1 Corinthians 13:9 NIV

2. 1 Corinthians 2:16 NIV

3. The Hebrew word in Psalm 139:24 is *'otseb,'* often translated as 'that which causes pain or sorrow.' It is frequently translated as the English word 'wicked.' A form of the English word 'wicker,' describing twisted twigs or branches, this term expresses a distorted way of thinking that grieves the heart of God.

4. Genesis 2:18 NIV

5. 2 Timothy 2:15 NASB

6. Psalm 25:4 NIV

7. Cunningham, *Why Not Women*, 229.

8. Ecclesiastes 4:9 NIV

CHAPTER 13
Your Story

1. Proverbs 18:2 (My paraphrase)

CHAPTER 14
"Final Words"

1. Matthew 16:18 NIV

2. Ephesians 4:16 NASB

3. James 1:19 NIV

4. 1 Samuel 13:14 (My paraphrase)

5. Mark 3:17

6. Acts 4:36

7. Acts 2:1 NKJV

8. *KJV Dictionary and Concordance* (Nashville, TN: Holman Reference, 2007), 923.

9. John 17:21 NLT

Made in the USA
Columbia, SC
01 July 2025